the new
bead**weaving**

beading

These studies which stimulate the young, divert the old, are an ornament in prosperity and a refuge and comfort in adversity; they delight us at home, are no impediment in public life, keep us company at night, in our travels, and whenever we retire to the country.

— Marcus Tullius Cicero (106–43 B.C.), Roman orator, philosopher, statesman.

the new
beadweaving
great projects with
innovative materials

ann benson

...rling Publishing Co., Inc. New York

A Sterling/Chapelle Book

chapelle, ltd. I

Jo Packham
Sara Toliver
Cindy Stoeckl

Editor: Leslie Farmer
Photography: Kevin Dilley for Hazen Photography
Photo Stylists: Connie Duran, Suzy Skadburg
Art Director: Karl Haberstich
Copy Editor: Marilyn Goff
Staff: Kelly Ashkettle, Areta Bingham, Donna Chambers,
        Ray Cornia, Emily Frandsen, Lana Hall, MacKenzie Johnson,
        Susan Jorgensen, Jennifer Luman, Melissa Maynard,
        Barbara Milburn, Lecia Monsen, Kim Taylor, Linda Venditti,
        Desirée Wybrow

Library of Congress Cataloging-in-Publication Data

Benson, Ann.
  New beadweaving : great projects with innovative materials / Ann Benson.
        p. cm.
  "A Sterling/Chapelle Book."
  ISBN 1-4027-0818-1
  1. Beadwork. 2. Jewelry making. I. Title.
TT860 .B485 2004
745.58'2--dc22

                                                    2003021844

10 9 8 7 6 5 4 3 2 1

Published by Sterling Publishing Co., Inc.
387 Park Avenue South, New York, NY 10016
©2004 by Ann Benson
Distributed in Canada by Sterling Publishing
c/o Canadian Manda Group, One Atlantic Avenue, Suite 105
Toronto, Ontario, Canada M6K 3E7
Distributed in Great Britain by Chrysalis Books
64 Brewery Road, London N7 9NT, England
Distributed in Australia by Capricorn Link (Australia) Pty. Ltd.
P.O. Box 704, Windsor, NSW 2756, Australia
Printed in China
All Rights Reserved

Sterling ISBN 1-4027-0818-1

write us

If you have questions or comments, please contact:
  Chapelle, Ltd., Inc.,
  P.O. Box 9252, Ogden, UT 84409
  (801) 621-2777 • (801) 621-2788 Fax
  e-mail: chapelle@chapelleltd.com
  web site: chapelleltd.com

contents

getting started

8	beads
12	thread
13	tools
13	jewelry components
13	beading tips

surface beading

16	surface-beading primer
20	the lovers
22	irish sunset
25	medieval castle
29	dimensional sunflowers

filet beading

32	filet-beading primer
36	coaster
38	heart ornament
40	black lace necklace
43	bridal bag

the new beadweaving

ladder bead-weaving

50   ladder bead-weaving primer

51   bridal necklace

54   bugle earrings

56   pyramids bracelet

58   rainbow bracelet

loom bead-weaving

62   loom bead-weaving primer

64   kilim rug

70   camellias

76   garden sunset

81   kimono

needle-weaving

88   needle-weaving primer

92   bargello bookmark

94   triangle necklace

96   wave pendant

99   hex beaded necklace

102   egyptian brooch

104   turquoise combination

108   pink crystals necklace

114   needle cases
       diamond needle case
       watercolor needle case

122   bargello lamp shade

in the back

127   metric equivalency chart

127   index

beads

seed beads

Most of us are familiar with these small beads that are often used in traditional Native American jewelry. They are round or oval in shape and have a centered hole.

Seed beads are made of glass that is heated to a molten state. Generally, the beads are colored when metals and other chemicals are infused into the molten mixture. The molten glass is extruded to form beads. When cooled, the beads are sorted for size, from 15o (very tiny) to 6o (the largest seed bead).

There are no standard packages for beads. Each company that sells beads to an individual consumer has its own put-up size.

delica seed beads

Delica seed beads are also quite small, corresponding roughly to 11o seed bead size. The beads are extruded to have a large hole and thin wall, and the shape is tubular. They are excellent for needle-weaving techniques such as the brick stitch on page 88 and the peyote stitch on page 91, because of their consistency in size and shape and because their large holes will accommodate several passes of thread (which is necessary in some weaving techniques). Delicas are readily available in a very wide range of colors and finishes.

hex seed beads

Hex seed beads are six-sided extruded beads with very large holes and very thin walls. They are similar in size to delicas, but the range of colors and finishes is quite a bit more limited. They also are excellent for weaving and are not too difficult to find.

three-cut seed beads

Three-cut seed beads come in two sizes, 12o and 9o. They are literally cut after extrusion to form the flat shiny surfaces that give them a faceted look. The range of colors and finishes is extremely limited, but three-cuts are widely used nevertheless—they are favored

11o Standard Seed Beads

#2 Bugle

12o Three-cut Seed Beads

#3 Bugle

6o Large Pebble Seed Beads

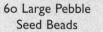

#5 Bugle

Hex Seed Beads

10mm Bugle

Delica Seed Beads

18mm Bugle

25mm Bugle

Fancy Glass Beads

Faceted Crystal Beads

Metal Beads

Cloisonné Beads

on elegant evening clothes because of their extreme sparkle and shine.

Note: The holes may be inconsistent, so buy more than you think you will need as a good percentage might be unusable.

bugle beads

Bugle beads are long narrow beads with a centered hole running the length of the bead. They range from #1 (approximately 2mm long) to 25mm (roughly 1"). Occasionally, bugle beads can be found in even longer lengths, but availability is very inconsistent. The most popular sizes to work with are #2 (4mm), #3 (6mm), and #5 (12mm). Generally, bugle beads are used to embellish a design mainly worked in seed beads. Bugle beads work especially well in hand- or loom-woven designs.

fancy glass beads

Available in so many varieties, it is impossible to describe all of the fancy glass beads. Most bead stores and mail-order catalogs will have hundreds of different styles, and most of those styles will come in a range of colors and finishes. Some are merely one color of glass formed into a ball with a beading hole, while others may also incorporate precious metal foils or threads of colored glass.

faceted crystal beads

These cut-crystal beads have a wonderful diamond-like fire when light-struck. They are made of fine quality glass (usually with a high lead content) and are shaped by a mechanized cutting process. They are extremely expensive but readily available.

Cut-crystal beads are available in many shapes and sizes, from 4mm cone-shaped beads to 18mm ovals. They are available in a good range of colors (mostly transparent).

metal beads

Metal beads give a piece a finished look. They are available either smooth or molded and have shiny, brushed, and antiqued metallic finishes.

cloisonné beads

These beads are often handcrafted and lend a very dramatic look to your piece. They can be used as the focal point in the design or as an accent.

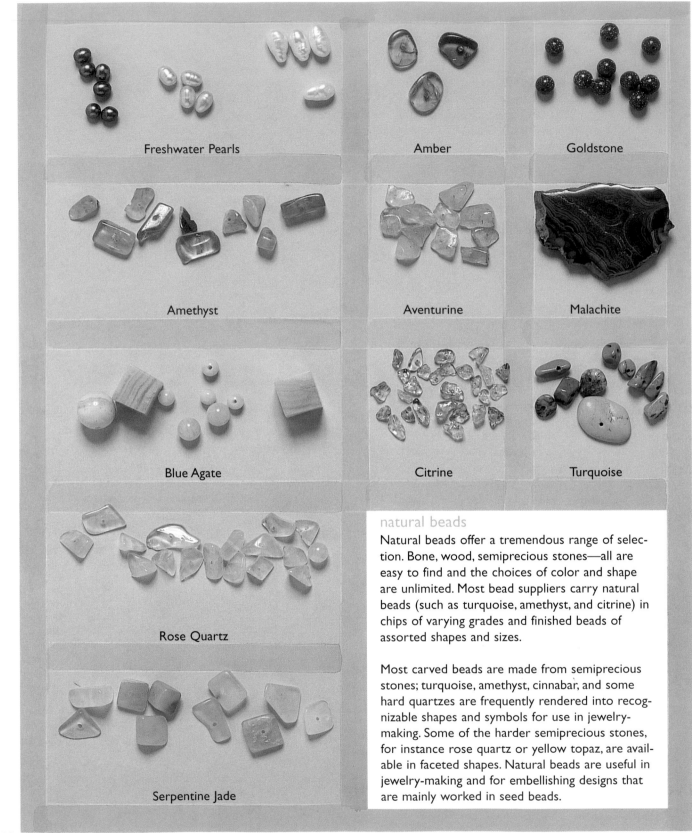

Freshwater Pearls

Amber

Goldstone

Amethyst

Aventurine

Malachite

Blue Agate

Citrine

Turquoise

Rose Quartz

Serpentine Jade

natural beads

Natural beads offer a tremendous range of selection. Bone, wood, semiprecious stones—all are easy to find and the choices of color and shape are unlimited. Most bead suppliers carry natural beads (such as turquoise, amethyst, and citrine) in chips of varying grades and finished beads of assorted shapes and sizes.

Most carved beads are made from semiprecious stones; turquoise, amethyst, cinnabar, and some hard quartzes are frequently rendered into recognizable shapes and symbols for use in jewelry-making. Some of the harder semiprecious stones, for instance rose quartz or yellow topaz, are available in faceted shapes. Natural beads are useful in jewelry-making and for embellishing designs that are mainly worked in seed beads.

bead colors

The glass used to create seed beads is colored with chemicals and molten metals. Because the coloring agents become part of the glass itself, most beads are extremely colorfast and will wash well. There are two major exceptions to this rule, notably dyed beads, where the color is "fused" to the outer surface of the bead, and galvanized beads, where the metallic finish is applied to the glass surface. Dyed and galvanized beads should not be used in anything that will require regular washing.

Beads with colors that appear solid are the best choice for use in most projects. There are several different types of solid-colored beads, such as opaque, matte opaque, lined, galvanized, Ceylon, opaque lustered, and matte transparent which do not look transparent.

Transparent beads are not suitable for most projects for two reasons: 1) the thread is visible inside them; and 2) the color of the background used for surface beading will show through.

The range of colors in a "family" of beads is quite limited. If you get five shades of one color, you are lucky!

Because of the limited chemical process used to create the bead colors, there are only so many variations available. In certain shades, such as the yellow family and the olive greens, the limitations are more severe. However, with a little creativity, a limited color palette may span further than you might expect.

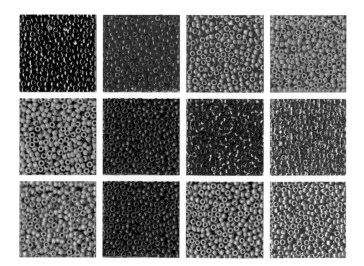

figuring needed amounts

Seed beads and delica beads are sold by metric weights, i.e., grams and portions of kilograms. Packet sizes vary from one vendor to the next—one company may sell a 7.5 gram tube of a particular color, while another company sells a 10 gram plastic bag of the same color. More expensive beads, such as those with 24-karat gold finish, may be sold in amounts as small as 3 grams per pack. Use the numbers indicated in the materials list for each project and the guidelines below to figure the amounts you will need to purchase.

Size 11o seed beads can be purchased in tubes, plastic bag packs, and hanks (Czech beads). Japanese beads are not sold in hanks.

1 gram = 100 beads
1 teaspoon = 5 grams = 500 beads
12 hanks = approximately .5 kilogram
1 hank = approximately 4000 beads

Size 15o seed beads are generally sold in 20–40 gram packages at retail. They can also be purchased in larger amounts, usually 100 grams or 250 grams.

1 gram = 220 beads
1 teaspoon = 5 grams = 1100 beads

Delica beads can be purchased in tubes and plastic bag packs.

1 gram = 200 beads
1 teaspoon = 5 grams = 1000 beads

These are rough equivalents; there can be some variance in the number of beads per gram, depending on the finish and color of the bead.

In general, beads with metallic finishes (iris, galvanized) are heavier than unfinished beads, thus there are fewer beads per gram. Beads with matte finishes have had some of their surface taken off in processing and are minutely lighter, so there are more beads per gram.

Another consideration is the inevitable presence of "blem" beads, those that are misshapen or broken, and therefore unusable. A safe rule of thumb is to buy 15% more than you think you will need.

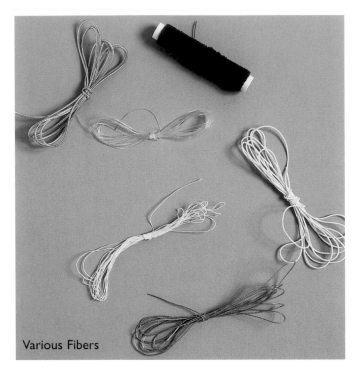

Various Fibers

thread

choosing a fiber

For stringing beads, almost any kind of flexible thread or cord can be used, providing the holes of the beads will accommodate the thread's diameter.

A fiber of an appropriate weight is essential for a nice presentation. For example, very heavy beads must be strung on a substantial fiber, such as elastic, heavy nylon, perle cotton, or multifilament rayon. Nylon monofilament, which is similar to fishing line, is also a good choice for projects with a good deal of weight.

When choosing a fiber, consider the drape of your project. For example, if you are working a necklace and want the necklace to move freely, lightweight silk or nylon, perhaps doubled for strength, is a good choice. But if you want the necklace to take on a defined shape, or to curve predictably, you should use a lightweight twisted wire or nylon monofilament.

For beading on surfaces, needle-weaving, and weaving on a loom, ordinary sewing thread is used most often. A neutral or coordinating color looks best.

In many cases, the thread or cord will be stiff enough to slip through a bead's hole without the use of a needle. However, lighter weight fibers require the use of a needle. Choosing a needle can be tricky as the eye of the needle must accommodate the thread and still pass through the bead. Another option is to use tape to form a "shoelace" end. This will pass through the holes of many larger beads.

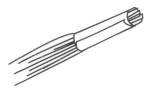

Tape fiber ends to form a "shoelace" end.

length of thread

Unless otherwise indicated, cut a 24"–30" length of thread to begin the project. Thread the needle. Slip beads on needle and work beading design, according to project instructions.

Note: A longer thread tends to tangle, and a shorter thread necessitates frequent threadings.

adding a new length of thread

When approximately 3" of thread remain unbeaded on the needle and the design is not yet complete, it is time to add a new thread.

Remove the needle from the old thread and cut a new 24"–30" length. Thread the needle, leaving a 5" tail. Tie the end of the old thread and the end of the new thread in a square knot, positioning the knot about 1" from the last bead.

Place a tiny dot of glue on the knot. Wipe off any excess glue and continue beading as if one continuous thread were being used.

Note: The glue need not be dry before proceeding.

Allow the thread ends to protrude from the work until the new thread is well established within the design. Pull gently on the knotted ends and clip them close so that they disappear into the design.

tools

needles

Needles are essential for almost every project in this book. Make certain to have a good assortment of sharp needles on hand.

Beading needles are traditionally long and thin to accommodate many beads at one time. These needles are particularly useful when stringing strands of beads for bracelets, necklaces, and long fringes. Beading needles are also well suited to weaving on a loom as they can catch several beads at a time when making the return trip on the weft thread.

Traditional beading needles are not well suited for beading on surfaces or needle-weaving. The smaller #9 embroidery needle is ideal when working with seed beads size 11o or larger. For finely drilled stones and pearls, a #10 between needle is recommended.

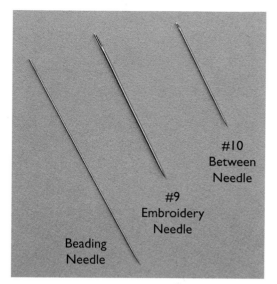

#10
Between
Needle

#9
Embroidery
Needle

Beading
Needle

pliers & wire cutters

Several projects require the use of pliers and wire cutters. Round-nosed pliers are used mainly for forming loops in wire eye pins and head pins. Needle-nosed pliers are used for closing loops, flattening and closing crimps, and attaching rings. Wire cutters are used for trimming head pins, eye pins, and beading wire.

You need not make a special trip to the craft store to purchase these tools as they are commonly found in most hardware stores. As you become more involved in beading as a needle art, you may require more specialized tools for accomplishing the more difficult techniques. In such cases, there are some very fine bead mail-order companies that can accommodate your needs.

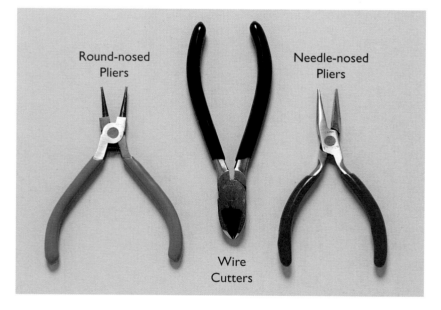

Round-nosed
Pliers

Needle-nosed
Pliers

Wire
Cutters

jewelry components

It is easy to make beautiful beaded accessories using jewelry components, also known as "findings." Some strung beadwork (open-ended strands, as opposed to continuous loops) will require a component—in most cases, a clasp. Following is an overview of the various sorts of components and their uses.

crimps

Crimps are small metal tubes that are crushed with pliers or a specific crimping tool to hold wires or cords together. They are useful in attaching clasps to necklaces made of wire.

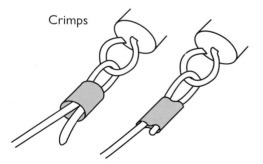

Crimps

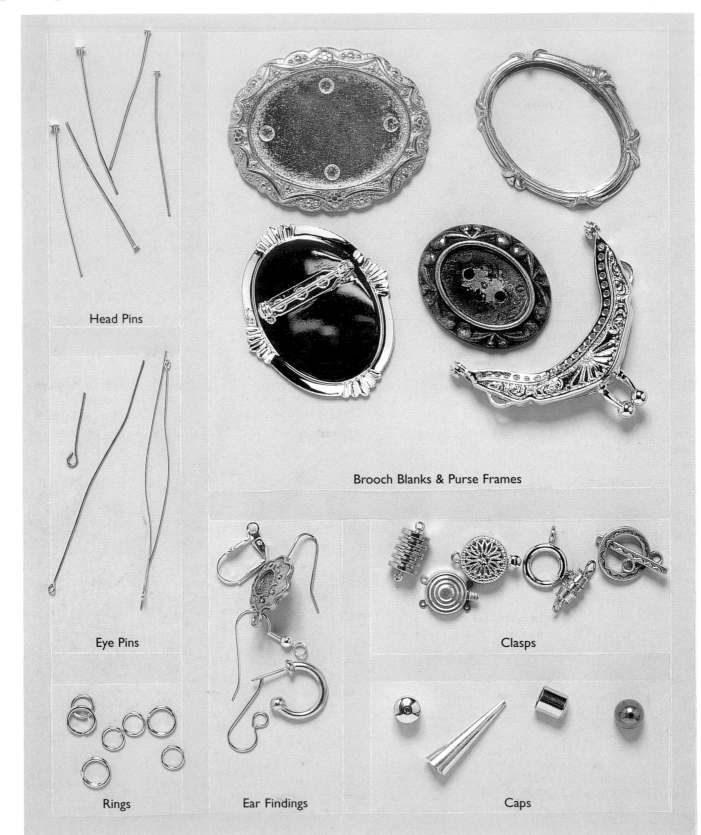

Head Pins

Brooch Blanks & Purse Frames

Eye Pins

Clasps

Rings

Ear Findings

Caps

head pins

Head pins are used to attach beads to other types of components such as ear wires and necklace blanks. They are long rigid wires with one end flattened to prevent the bead from slipping off.

eye pins

Eye pins are similar to head pins but instead of a flattened end, there is a loop on one end to which a head pin might be attached.

rings

Rings are often used to attach beads mounted on head pins or eye pins to another component. Rings are also used to form the end of a necklace to which a one-sided clasp such as a claw clasp has been attached. Rings allow free movement of a dropped head pin, which would otherwise be restricted in its movement to one direction.

brooch blanks

Brooch blanks are formed metal shapes (some with pin backs already attached) on which beadwork may be mounted. Some blanks that would ordinarily be used to hold a single large cabochon (an oval stone with a flat back, usually of a semiprecious stone such as turquoise or rose quartz) can be used for small pieces of beadwork.

purse frames

Purse frames are also made of formed metal and are available in a variety of finishes. These are a very effective type of closure for needle-woven bags.

ear findings

Ear findings are available in a wide assortment of styles and types, from simple wires to preformed ear studs with loops for attaching beads.

Note: Clip-on earrings are easy to find for those who do not have pierced ears.

clasps

Clasps are used to close bead strands. Most clasps are two-part metal units that open and close. There are many different types of clasps, some quite decorative; such clasps can become an element of design as opposed to a piece of hardware.

caps

Caps are used to finish a string or multiple strings of beads. Caps are cylindrical or conical, made of metal, and contain an eye pin. The completed string(s) of beads is knotted onto the eye pin and covered with the cap. The remaining end of the eye pin is then attached to a clasp or ring.

beading tips

spilled beads

There is no use crying over spilled beads. Instead, put a new bag in your vacuum cleaner and vacuum them up. If only a few beads spilled, wet the tip of your finger to pick them up.

jumping beads

If you store your beads in a plastic bag, they will probably try to jump out when you open it. Blow into the bag lightly and the moisture from your breath will settle the beads enough to pour them out.

counting beads

It is very tempting when weaving to loop away without recounting your beads after threading on a very long row—but you will only do this once. If you have to remove a row, first pull the needle off the thread. Then use the tip of the needle to gently pull the thread out of the beads.

organization

A practical way of organizing your materials is found in using small acrylic boxes to hold beads of a color and size. Place these boxes in a larger utility box within reach together with beading and sewing needles, findings, scissors, etc.

removing beads

If you accidentally sew on the wrong color or a misshapen bead, or if the work is puckering, remove the offending bead by breaking it off with needle-nosed pliers. Close your eyes and look away as the bead breaks.

surface-beading primer

Surface beading is simple and quick to do, versatile, and holds its shape without elaborate finishing.

In this technique, beads are sewn directly onto card stock or nonwoven fabric, following a printed design for precise placement. The design printed on the surface combines graphic lines and symbols to indicate bead placement.

card stock versus nonwoven fabric

The methods employed for beading on card stock are essentially the same as those used for beading on nonwoven fabric. The main difference is in the ease of finishing—card-beading pieces hold their shape without the additional support required by fabric.

methods for transferring the design

When beading on card stock, the best method for transferring a design is to photocopy it directly onto the card stock.

For beading on fabric, you can transfer the design onto the fabric in one of two ways. The first is to trace the design directly from this book, using a transfer pencil to draw your design onto paper first. Iron the traced design onto the fabric surface.

Note: Remember that the design must initially be reversed, or it will come out in mirror image.

Then a rough color representation of the design can be painted directly onto the fabric. Permanent color fabric markers, sold in most commercial fabric and craft stores, are excellent for use in applying color to fabric. The color selection is limited, however, and it can be an expensive undertaking, depending on the number of colors being used in the design.

A second and favorite method of applying color to a stiff nonwoven fabric is to scan the design using a color scanner and a computer and print the color directly from the computer printer onto the fabric.

Simply set the printer in the card stock position to accommodate the thickness of the fabric, then print.

sewing on seed beads

Use a single strand of neutral color ordinary sewing thread and a small sharp needle such as a #10 or #11 "between." When filling large single color areas such as background, you can match the thread color to the beads. Before beginning, trim excess card to ½" (1.2cm) all around.

Seed beads (11o, 15o, and Delicas) are the most commonly used type of bead in card-beading. They can be sewn on individually, in groups of two or three, or in long continuous rows that cover an area.

Single beads are used to fill small spaces. The thread is brought up through the card, the bead is slipped onto the needle, then the needle is pushed back through the card as shown.

When you are sewing the beads onto an outer edge or along a curve, they should be sewn on in groups of two or

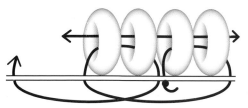

three as shown. Notice the second thread that runs through the entire group; this is called "backtracking." The backtracking thread stabilizes and smooths the line.

Following the design, pierce holes in the line you intend to cover, using beads threaded on a needle to judge the approximate distance as shown. This will facilitate the proper placement of beads on a line.

This photo shows a curved line of beads; the line on the left has no backtracking thread. The line on the right is smoothed by the addition of a backtracking thread, so the overall appearance is improved.

Long rows of seed beads may also be sewn on to fill large areas such as background and foreground. Thread multiple beads, up to 12 at one time, onto the needle and fit them into the intended space as shown (top and lower left). Loosely secure the entire row by inserting the needle back through the card at the row's end (middle right). Then pierce holes at intervals of two or three beads, just to one side or the other of the row. The row is secured with a "tie-down" or "couching" thread (lower right).

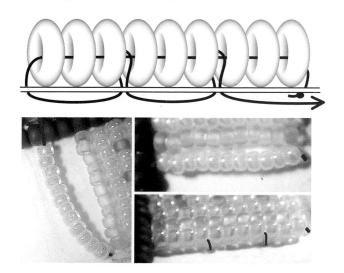

The photo at right shows a row with too many beads for a proper fit in the intended space. One bead should be slipped off the needle before the thread is passed through the surface.

The photo at right shows a row with too few beads to fit properly. One bead should be added before the thread is passed through the surface.

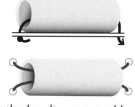

Delica beads and hex beads can be sewn on the card in the same manner as regular oval seed beads.

bugle beads

Bugle beads are elongated tubes; they come in many different lengths. Sew them in place as shown (top). The holes are usually large but the cut edges of the beads are sharp, so you may want to use a doubled thread to secure them, as a single thread may fray. If there is too much movement in the bead, you can add a second thread as shown in the overhead view (bottom). This is sometimes necessary with longer bugle beads.

larger seed beads

Larger seed beads such as sizes 6o and 8o can be treated as regular seed beads if that is what the design calls for. They can also be used decoratively with anchors as shown. For 6o beads, 11o beads should be used for anchoring. For 8o beads, use 15o beads for anchoring.

semiprecious-stone chips

Semiprecious-stone chips are odd shaped, but often have one side that is relatively flat. The holes may be quite small. Place the flatter side against the card and anchor the chip in place with a seed bead, either 11o or 15o depending on the relative size of

the chip. In some cases, the hole may run from end to end, especially if the chip is of very fine quality. In that case, treat the chip as a pearl.

freshwater pearls

Freshwater pearls (rice shaped) should be laid with the flatter edge against the card as shown unless otherwise indicated in the specific directions. They often have very small holes; a fine needle should be used. Other shapes of pearls, especially those with short holes, can be anchored with small seed beads, similar to chips or larger seed beads.

crystals and other faceted beads

Crystals and other faceted beads should be sewn with two threads if the holes are placed parallel to the card. In the overhead view (top), the holes in the card are exaggerated for visibility. Depending on the number of facets on the bead you are using, they may not lie perfectly flat. Having two separate threads will help minimize movement of the bead after it is sewn. Flatter crystals can be treated with an anchoring bead (bottom), in a similar manner to larger seed beads or chips.

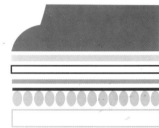

finishing surface beading

Finishing is simple. The basic concept is to fuse a fabric of choice onto the back of the finished beadwork, then trim away the excess card with small sharp scissors. Lightweight, tightly woven fabrics such as light felt, ultrasuede, and very lightweight leather are good choices. You can also use 100% cotton. Preshrink backing fabric by pressing it before beginning.

Ultrahold fusible web works well. Layer the components as shown and press together for five seconds. Reposition the iron and repeat so there will be no steam holes. Flip the piece over and iron close to the edge of the beads. Allow the piece to cool thoroughly before proceeding, as beads retain heat.

Iron

Clean white paper
Backing fabric
Fusible web (paper removed)
Beadwork, beads down
Clean white towel

Trim the excess card carefully using small scissors. If a fringe has been added to the finished beadwork, hold it aside while trimming and take care not to cut any threads.

Apply a thin line of diluted glue around the trimmed edges to secure the edge and prevent fraying.

If desired, you can glue a pin back onto the back of the piece. Sew through the holes on the pin back, bringing the thread to the front of the piece. Secure the thread and clip close.

Beads can be sewn onto the surface of leather as well as card stock or nonwoven fabric. In this piece, assorted beads and natural stones were chosen to accent the colored leather.

the lovers

putting beads

on the surface of card stock is easier than it looks. Just make certain to follow the pattern as closely as possible. Classical Greek sculpture was the inspiration for this design. It was stitched in white, black, and shades of gray to simulate the look of marble. Once complete, it was glued onto the lid of this letter box. The piece could also be set into a matted picture frame and used to decorate a wall or tabletop. There are many Greek and Roman architectural design elements available on the market that would blend nicely with this piece.

materials

Beads as listed in bead code
Card stock or nonwoven fabric:
white, 7" square
Thread: white

instructions

finished size: 5¼" x 6¼"

1 Refer to Methods for Transferring
the Design on page 16. Transfer the
The Lovers Design onto the card
stock or fabric.

2 Refer to the diagrams in the Surface-
beading Primer on pages 16–18
before beginning. Using those techniques, sew on beads, beginning with
the longer rows first, then fill in the
gaps with individual beads, turning
them in any direction to accommodate the specific space.

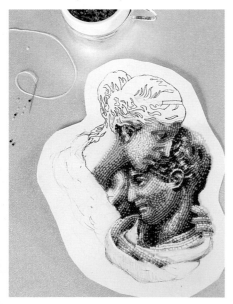

3 Finish as desired.

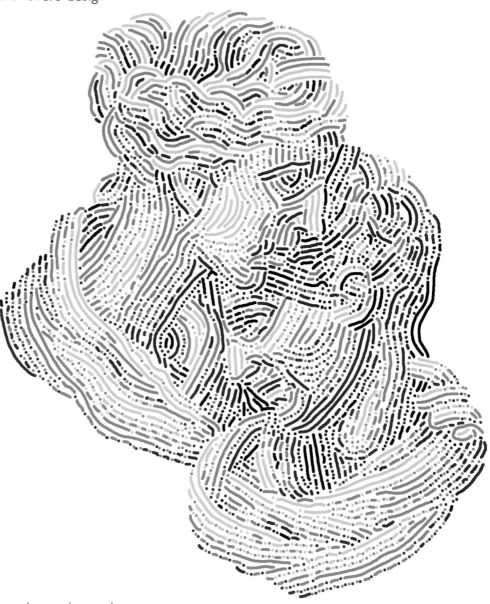

bead code

15o Seed beads:
  Miyuki 401 or Toho 49 opaque black (597 or 2 grams)

  Miyuki 425 lustered brown (1655 or 7 grams)

  Miyuki 526 or Toho 150 Ceylon gray (2150 or 9 grams)

  Miyuki 591 or Toho 121 lustered cream (1598 or 6 grams)

irish sunset

create extra dimension by incorporating pearls and stones into your design. They combine

perfectly with the natural colors selected for this piece. This scene, set on the shores of one of the world's most

beautiful islands, is enclosed by traditional Celtic knotted patterns. The piece reflects the Celtic theme that all

things—water, earth, trees, and the heavens—are connected.

bead code

15o Seed beads:

Miyuki 132FR matte light sand (497)

Miyuki 1052 or Toho 559 metallic gold (960)

Miyuki 457 or Toho 223 metallic bronze (170)

Miyuki 536 Ceylon aqua (328)

Miyuki 2075 matte deep blue (11)

Miyuki 1486 opaque deep purple (18)

Miyuki 222A lined orchid (35)

Toho 959 lined rose (27)

Miyuki 539 or Toho 986 lined salmon (28)

Miyuki 2197 lined pale peach (26)

Miyuki 134FR matte medium brown AB (105)

Miyuki 135F matte dark brown (82)

Toho 610 matte black (59)

Miyuki 520 or Toho 144 Ceylon pale green (37)

Miyuki 411 or Toho 47 opaque medium green (38).

Miyuki 431J opaque dark green (15)

Miyuki 2033 matte light olive (30)

Miyuki 524 or Toho 146 Ceylon pale blue (49)

Miyuki 149FR matte medium blue AB (69)

 Miyuki 470 or Toho 161 crystal AB (64)

 Turquoise chips (4)

Freshwater pearls, 4mm–5mm (4)

materials

Beads as listed in bead code
Card stock or nonwoven fabric:
   white, 4" square
Thread: white

instructions

finished size: 3¼" diameter

Note: There is a good deal of intricate stitchery in this design. If you are working on card, it may weaken from too many holes. Try to use previously pierced holes whenever possible, rather than adding more holes.

1 Refer to Methods for Transferring the Design on page 16. Transfer the Irish Sunset Design onto the card stock or nonwoven fabric.

irish sunset design

2 Refer to the diagrams in the Surface-beading Primer on pages 16–18 before beginning. Using those techniques, sew on beads in the following order:

a. Sew on the metallic gold and bronze seed beads for the border. On the outer edge, the beads are sewn on in groups of three. Run a stabilizing thread through the entire line when each segment is finished.

Note: When sewing on beads initially, discard any that do not slip easily over the needle; those beads may break when you introduce the second thread.

b. Sew on the light amber AB seed beads.

c. Sew on the turquoise chips, anchored with Ceylon aqua seed beads.

d. Sew on the pearls.

e. Sew on the Ceylon aqua seed beads to fill in the background around the turquoise and pearls, then fill in all the remaining border background areas.

f. Sew on the seed beads for the central design area, beginning with the rocks, shrubbery, and clouds. Add the sky, sand, and water.

3 Finish as desired.

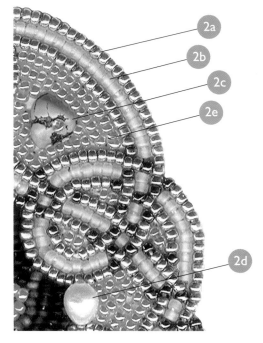

finished irish sunset

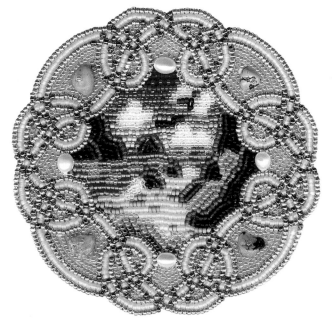

24

medieval castle

different-sized seed beads can create the illusion of depth and lend a stunning visual effect to your piece. In this piece, 11o seed beads are used to contrast with the smaller 15o beads and to illustrate the clumps of leaves on the tree boughs and bushes in the background and flower petals on flowers in the foreground. The beads are worked in different directions to make the various design elements stand apart from each other. Once complete, this piece was set into this purse frame and serves as a whimsical personal accessory.

bead code

15o Seed beads:
Miyuki 416A opaque light gray (365)

Miyuki 416 opaque medium gray (125)

Miyuki 526 or Toho 150 Ceylon gray (325)

Miyuki 524 opaque lustered garnet (163)

Miyuki 610 or Toho 49 opaque black (35)

Miyuki 421 or Toho 141 opaque lustered pearl (88)

Miyuki 426 or Toho 129 opaque lustered red (34)

Miyuki 534A Ceylon orchid (135)

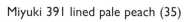
Miyuki 434 opaque lustered cobalt (80)

Miyuki 422A or Toho 402 opaque lustered lemon (109)

Miyuki 391 lined pale peach (35)

Miyuki 517 or Toho 145 Ceylon pink (32)

Miyuki 410A opaque lustered rose (60)

Miyuki 417A opaque Sioux blue (517)

Miyuki 412E or Toho 53 opaque medium aqua (158)

Miyuki 413 or Toho 43 opaque light aqua (89)

Miyuki 430D opaque lustered light sapphire (154)

Miyuki 430M opaque lustered
        medium mint green (436)

Miyuki 331 or Toho 179 transparent
        forest green AB (278)

Freshwater pearls, 3.8mm–4.4mm
        round or rice-shaped (10)

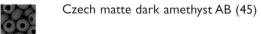
11o Seed beads:
Czech opaque lime (57)

Czech opaque light green (137)

Czech opaque medium green (120)

Czech opaque dark green (98)

Czech matte dark amethyst AB (45)

Czech matte medium amethyst AB (43)

Czech matte light amethyst (70)

Czech matte light green AB (75)

Czech matte emerald AB (10)

Miyuki 539 Ceylon rose (20)

Miyuki 1937 lined tangerine (20)

Czech Ceylon pale orchid (21)

Miyuki 1931 lined rose (22)

Miyuki 1935 lined salmon (21)

Czech opaque rust (28)

materials

> Beads as listed in bead code
> Interfacing-type fabric, heavy-weight,
>   nonwoven: white, 6" square
> Thread: off-white

medieval castle design

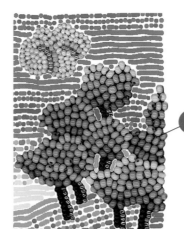

a. Sew on the seed beads for the trees and cloud. Beads are sewn on two or three at a time to form the leaves.

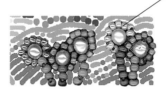

b. Sew on the pearls, then surround the pearls with seed beads to create the flowers. Run a second stabilizing thread through the seed beads surrounding the pearls to smooth out the circular shape.

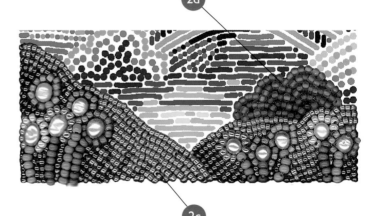

instructions

finished size 3¼" x 4¼"

1 Refer to Methods for Transferring the Design on page 16. Transfer the Medieval Castle Design onto the fabric.

2 Refer to the diagrams in the Surface-beading Primer on pages 16–18 before beginning. Using those techniques, sew on beads in the following order:

c. Sew on the 150 seed beads for the foreground, working around the flowers while maintaining a sloped effect, which creates the "grassy" area.

d. Add the "shrub" area on the right side, above the grassy area with flowers.

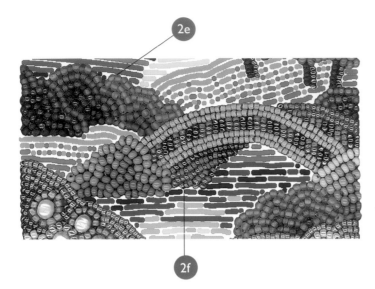

e. Add the shrub areas in the midsection.

f. Add the bridge, working the long, light gray curved lines first to establish the shape.

g. Add the castle, working the light gray beads in the arched windows first to establish their shape; run a second stabilizing thread through the arches. Next, work the long straight rows.

h. Add the ramparts and flags. Sew on the beads of the flags two at a time and run a stabilizing thread through them.

i. After the foreground items have all been stitched, sew on the !5o beads for the water area, the grassy slope behind the trees, and the sky. It is OK if the rows in these areas are not perfectly straight; part of the charm of the design is the slight imperfection of the bead placement.

finished medieval castle

3 Finish as desired.

dimensional sunflowers

when beading

a surface, do not assume that it must remain flat. There are several ways to add dimension to the surface and make it come to life. In this piece, loops of 15o seed beads are used to create the raised texture of the sunflower petals. They are free-moving and encourage you to touch them—just to make certain they are not real! You can finish this cheerful piece with a beaded hanger and attach it to a gift; or you can glue on a pin back to create a wearable piece of art for yourself or for someone you know.

bead code

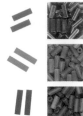 #2 Czech bugles:
silver-lined medium green AB (18)

matte light amethyst AB (59)

matte medium amethyst AB (25)

 11o Seed beads:
Czech matte amethyst (49)

Toho 557F matte galvanized gold (477)

8o Czech beads:
opaque cream (81)

opaque light blue (57)

15o Seed beads:
Miyuki 2075 matte dark blue (874)

Miyuki 431 or Toho 130 opaque lustered
medium green (178)

Miyuki 520 or Toho 144 Ceylon light green (200)

Miyuki 1479 opaque dyed pumpkin (432)

Miyuki 2238 lined gold (242)

Miyuki 135FR matte pale amber AB (286)

Miyuki 524 or Toho 146 Ceylon light blue (110)

Miyuki 591 or Toho 122 lustered cream (283)

dimensional sunflowers design

materials

Beads as listed in bead code
Card stock or nonwoven fabric:
  white, 5" square
Thread: white

instructions

finished size: 2¾" x 4"

1 Refer to Methods for Transferring the Design on page
16. Transfer the Dimensional Sunflowers Design onto
the card stock or nonwoven fabric.

2 Refer to the diagrams in the Surface-beading Primer
on pages 16–19 before beginning. Using those techniques, sew on beads in the following order:

d. Sew on the beads for the border. Create curved, straight, and corner areas. The outer and inner edges of the gold area are treated as lines; sew on no more than two beads at a time. To smooth the appearance, run a stabilizing thread through the entire line. Add the 8o light blue beads anchored with 15o light blue beads, then work the two-bead sections of gold between them.

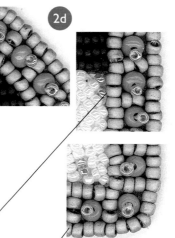

a. Sew on the beads for the vase. Sew on three lines of 11o matte amethyst seed beads, then add the matte amethyst and light amethyst bugles. Find a short bugle bead in the mix to fill in where the leaf tip meets the bugles; if necessary, work the leaf tip over that bugle. To smooth lines of bugles in the vase, run an additional stabilizing thread through the entire length of each line.

b. Sew on 8o cream beads for the flower centers. Outline each of the five full circles, then fill in the center. For the clusters of three, sew on each bead individually.

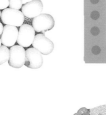

c. Sew on the beads for the leaves. Sew on medium green bugles to form the centers of the leaves. Add strands of 15o beads starting at the center of the leaf. Each strand starts with the medium green and blends to the light green.

Note: Check the fit of each strand before running the needle back through the card or fabric; the strand should be slightly longer than the required distance so it "puffs" up a bit to create texture.

e. Sew on the beads for the background and the tablecloth. Refer to the couching technique on page 17. Work the background in horizontal rows as much as possible, with single-bead fill-ins as needed. Work the three-bead clusters in the tablecloth with 15o light blue beads, then fill in around them with 15o cream beads in random directions.

f. Create flower petals with 15o beads, following the Petal Diagrams. Bring the needle up through the colored dot, thread on the beads, then reinsert the needle through the same hole in the card.

petal diagrams

Notes: Avoid pulling the thread too tightly. The base of each petal should sit against the surface of the card or fabric, yet still retain movement.

Follow the color coding for placement of petals. Notice that the dots are exaggerated in the diagram.

3 Finish as desired.

filet-beading primer

If you're familiar with filet crochet, you'll understand filet beading. The best choice of beads is 15o Japanese seed beads—the patterns emerge quite clearly with this size. The 11o's may also be used with great success, but Delicas are not recommended. Any filet crochet pattern can be adapted for use with beads. Here's how you can use your grandmother's patterns in a new way.

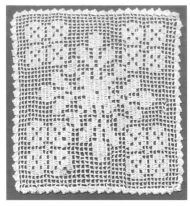

filet beading chart

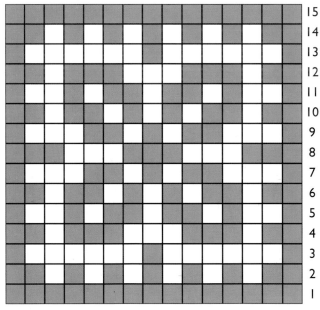

15
14
13
12
11
10
9
8
7
6
5
4
3
2
1

Similar to filet crochet, charts are shown in dark and light squares. Dark squares represent filled patterns (hereinafter referred to as "pats"). Light squares represent unfilled pats. Designs are counted from the bottom row upward, in horizontal rows, working as charted from right to left.

Use a #12 tapestry beading needle and lightweight nylon or machine-quilting thread.

Note: In the diagrams, some beads have colored dots; those correspond to the colored dots on the photos throughout the directions.

create the foundation row

Thread the needle with a 36" length of thread. Place a "stopper" bead (blue dot) on one end (it will be removed later), leaving a 6" tail of thread for later adjustments. Tape the stopper-bead end of the thread to a flat surface; the tape can be removed after a few rows when the weave stabilizes. Determine the total number of patterns (pats) in the bottom row of the chart, then add beads as shown in Illustration A to serve as their foundation according to the following formula:

(4 x total # of pats) beads + ! bead

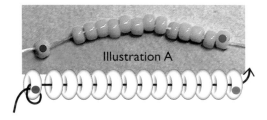

Illustration A

if the first pat is open

Add 11 beads. Skip 13 beads and run the needle through the 14th bead as shown in Illustration B. Run the needle through the last three beads—this forms one "leg" of the pat (indicated by the green line). Take up the slack, but do not pull too tightly, just enough to minimize the visibility of the thread within the beads. Run the needle through the back of the fourth bead to complete the open pat. Notice that in the photo, the loop appears rounded. This condition will persist until the next row is completed.

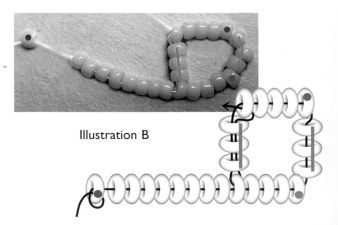

Illustration B

if the first pat is filled

Add nine beads after the foundation. Skip the first 11 beads on the thread, and run the needle through the 12th bead. Run the needle back through the last three beads in the loop, then take up the slack in the thread at this point. Run the needle through the back of the fourth bead as shown in Illustration C. This will stabilize this bead so it becomes the top bead of the center "leg" of a filled pat.

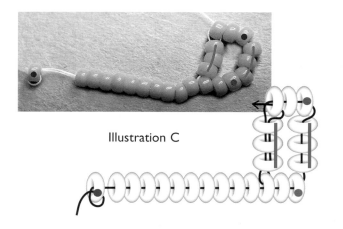

Illustration C

Slip five beads over the needle. Skip one bead on the foundation row, then run the needle and thread through the next bead. Run the needle back through the last three beads on the leg, take up the slack, then run the needle through the back of the fourth bead. This forms the third leg of the filled pat as shown in Illustration D.

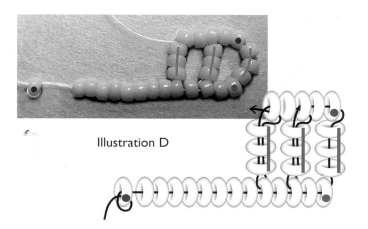

Illustration D

if the next pat is open

Add seven beads. Skip three beads on the foundation row and run the needle through the fourth bead as shown in Illustration E. Run the needle through the last three beads. This forms one "leg" of the pat (indicated by the green line). Run the thread through the back of the fourth bead (lighter blue dot), and you are in position to begin the next pat.

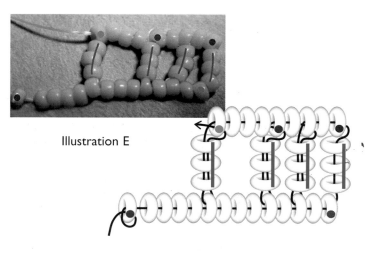

Illustration E

if the next pat is filled

Add five beads, skip the next bead on the foundation row, run the thread through the following bead as shown in Illustration F. Run the thread through the last three beads to form the leg; secure the leg by running the thread through the back of the fourth bead as in previous legs. Complete the pat by adding one more leg as shown in Illustration G.

Illustration F

Illustration G

the first row is complete

Shown in Illustration H is an example of a three-pat full row, consisting of two filled pats with an open pat between them. Of course, the beading itself will not look as neat as the diagrams, but as the rows progress, the appearance will become neater. You're now in position to begin the next row. The first step is to flip the work horizontally so the working thread is beginning at the right side of your chart and design.

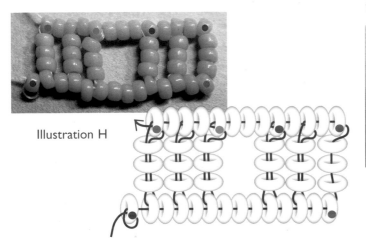

Illustration H

if the first pat in the new row is open

Add 11 beads as shown in Illustration I. Notice that beadwork has been flipped horizontally as previously described. Your thread emerges from the last bead in the top of the previous row (green dot). Skip the next three beads in the top of the previous row and run the needle through the fourth (light blue dot). Run the thread back through the last three added beads to create the leg. Run the thread through the back of the fourth bead to secure the leg.

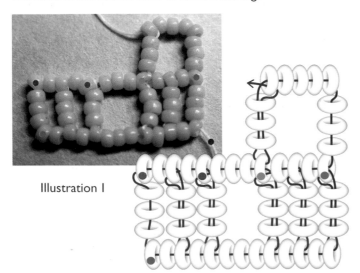

Illustration I

if the first pat in the new row is filled

Add nine beads as shown in Illustration J. Notice that the beadwork has been flipped horizontally as previously described. The thread emerges from the last bead in the top of the previous row (green dot). Skip one bead on the top of the previous row and run the thread through the next bead. Run the thread through the last three added beads to make the center leg of the filled pat, then through the back of the fourth bead to secure the leg.

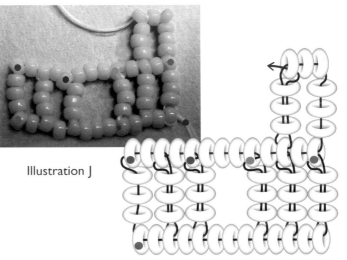

Illustration J

To complete the pat, work second leg as shown in Illustration K. Thread on five beads, skip one bead on the top of the previous row, then run the thread through the next bead (light blue dot). Run the thread through the last three added beads, then through the back of the fourth bead to secure the leg.

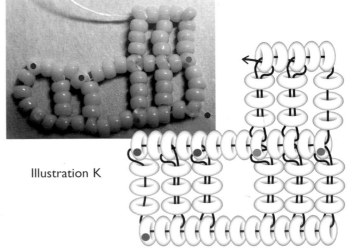

Illustration K

to complete the rows with filled and open pats

Review the diagrams and photos in "If the Next Pat is Open" and "If the Next Pat is Filled" on page 33. Work in horizontal rows as charted. Shown below are photos of next pats both open and filled.

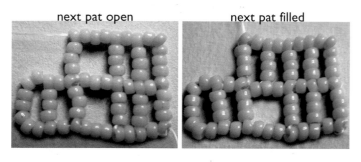

next pat open   next pat filled

filet-beading decreases

Decreases can be made at either end of a row. Illustration L shows a decrease of two pats on both sides of the row. On the right, simply run the thread back through the top beads in the previous row until the desired number of pats will be decreased (orange dot). At the left side of the row, simply stop making pats at the point where the desired number of pats will be decreased on that side (aqua dot).

Illustration L

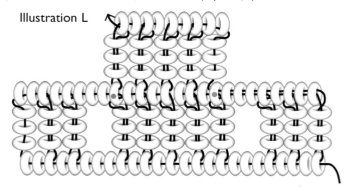

filet-beading increases

Increases may be added at either side of a row. To add pats at the right side as shown in Illustration M, thread on four beads (beyond the red dot bead) for each pat to be added.

Illustration M

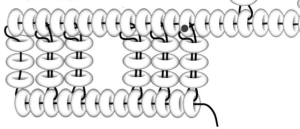

Proceed as if you were creating pats on the foundation row until the increase pats are added (sections 2 or 3, depending whether the pat is open or filled), then continue across the row as in section 4.

To add pats at the left side of a row, do not complete the last nonincrease leg (green stripe) as shown in Illustration N. Instead, bring the thread out in the last bead of the top of the previous row (pink dot) and add four beads for each pat of increase (orange stripe). Skip the last bead and run the thread back through all the orange stripe beads (creating a foundation row extension), then back through the pink dot bead and the green stripe beads. Run the thread through the back of the next bead to secure the leg. Proceed to add pats as in sections 2 or 3, depending on whether the pat is open or filled.

Illustration N

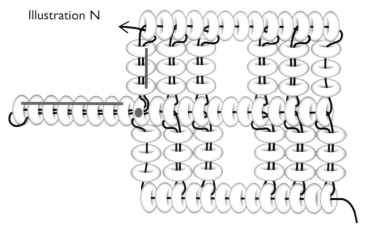

designs can be worked in rounds

Complete the foundation and the first row as if it were a flat pattern; but do not work the last leg of the final pat. Instead, attach the row to itself so the first and last legs are the same as shown in Illustration O. Run threads through the joining pats as needed until they are secure. Bring the thread out in the top bead of the common leg and run it through its own back to secure it, then proceed as if you were beginning a new row (sections 2 and 3).

Illustration O

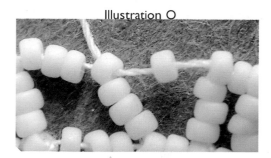

coaster

use filet stitch

patterns to create a beaded project. This square floral pattern is perfectly suited for creating an elegant coaster that is finished with a lace edge and felt backing. While the working of the design is intricate and needs to be done precisely, it becomes easy to do as you become familiar with pattern of the beads—knowing which patterns are open and which are closed. Make four or more coasters for a set. You can use them for a special occasion such as a bridal party, or simply place them on your coffee table to encourage everyday use.

materials

Beads
110 Seed beads: ivory (3 grams)

Other materials
Felt: navy, 4" square
Thread: off-white
Scissors

instructions

1 Refer to Filet-beading Primer on pages 32–35. Weave design according to Coaster Chart.

2 After completing the weave, add the lace around the edges as shown in the Coaster Lace Diagram.

3 Cut felt to the same size as the filet area. Do not include the lace in the measurement.

4 Position the felt so it backs the filet area but not the lace. Slip-stitch the felt in position with needle and thread.

coaster lace diagram

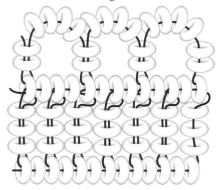

coaster chart

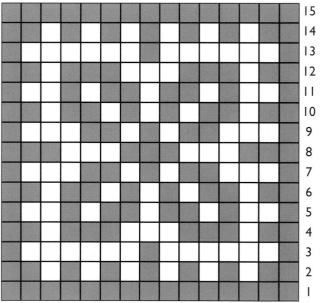

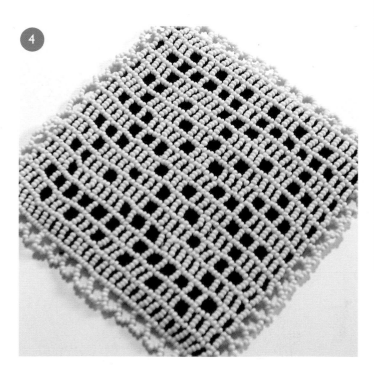

heart ornament

CREATE SHAPED PIECES by using increases and decreases in the pattern. This heart-shaped ornament begins at the bottom of the piece with one filled pattern and multiplies with each subsequent row until it evens out in the middle section. Then it begins decreasing the number of patterns to form the heart's lobes. It is finished with a beaded hanger.

heart ornament chart

17
16
15
14
13
12
11
10
9
8
7
6
5
4
3
2
1

materials

Beads
15o Seed beads: Miyuki 415C pink (3 grams)

Other materials
Paper towels
Thread: pink
Waxed paper
White glue

instructions

1 Refer to Filet-beading Primer on pages 32–35. Weave design according to Heart Ornament Chart, working increases and decreases as charted.

2 After completing the weave, bring the thread out in the center of the top of one side of the heart. Thread on enough beads to form a 2½" strand. Run the thread through the top of three beads on the center of the other side at the top of the heart. Add five beads; skip the last five beads on the 2½" strand, then run the thread back through all but the last five beads on the strand. Add five beads; run the thread back into the top on that side of the heart. Secure the thread within the weave and trim.

3 To stiffen, wet the entire piece and pat off the excess water with paper towels. Dilute white glue 1:1 with water. Soak the heart section (not the hanger strand) in the diluted glue and pat off the excess with paper towels. Lay the wet piece on waxed paper; straighten it if needed and allow it to dry.

bead tip

Create your own heart ornament design, using the Heart Ornament Blank. Simply fill in the squares as desired and work the filet design with beads of your choice.

heart ornament blank

black lace necklace

filet beading

thoughtfully combined with bead stringing makes an elegant necklace. This pattern is a combination of increases and stepped out decreases with a blossom design in the center. It is finished with beaded drops placed at each step along the bottom edge. Long beaded strands are attached to the top and joined by a silver clasp to form the necklace. Wear this piece with a solid-colored blouse or dress that has clean lines that do not compete with the lines in the necklace.

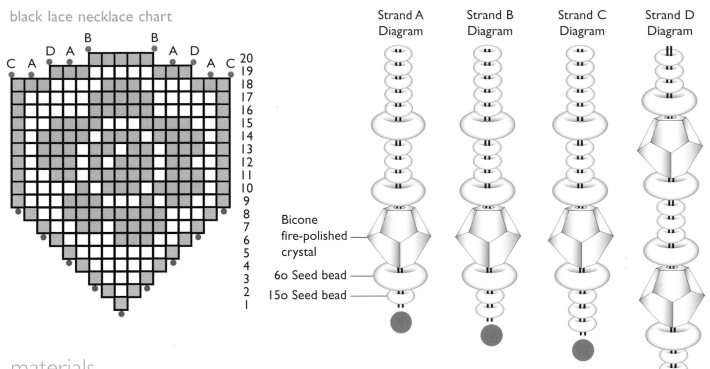

black lace necklace chart

Strand A Diagram Strand B Diagram Strand C Diagram Strand D Diagram

Bicone fire-polished crystal

6o Seed bead

15o Seed bead

materials

Beads
Bicone fire-polished crystals, black, 6mm (12)
15o Seed beads: opaque black (3 grams)
6o Seed beads: opaque black (41)
Teardrop fire-polished crystals, black, 7mm x 10mm (9)

Other materials
Clasp: silver
Thread: black
White glue

instructions

1 Refer to Filet-beading Primer on pages 32–35. Weave design according to Black Lace Necklace Chart, working increases and decreases as charted.

2 After completing the weave, add necklace strands.

a. Tie a new length of thread to the thread tail left from the beginning of the piece. Bring it out at the farthest outside letter on the chart, on either side. This will form the first of 10 necklace strands (five on each side), which will extend symmetrically from the top of the woven piece.

b. Thread on the crystals and seed beads, following the Strand C Diagram, working from the bottom (at the pink dot) up; thereafter, thread on 15o seed beads until the length of the strand is 8½". Take the thread through the loop of the clasp and back into the 15o seed beads. Run the thread back through the entire necklace strand, then work it through the weave so it emerges at the next letter on the chart (A).

c. Following the Strand A Diagram for this strand, repeat as for Strand C. Continue in this manner for the remaining strands on this side, also following Strand D Diagram and Strand B Diagram.

d. When all are complete, loop the excess thread invisibly into the weave and trim it close, adding a tiny drop of glue at the last loop.

3 Repeat Step 2 for the remaining strands on the other side of the weave.

4 Add the fringes at the base of the necklace at the locations (blue dots) marked on the chart, following the Necklace Drop Diagram and working the thread through the weave so it emerges at the next location on the chart. When all are complete, loop the excess thread invisibly into the weave and trim it close, adding a tiny drop of glue at the last loop.

bead tip

Create your own heart ornament design, using the Black Lace Necklace Blank. Simply fill in the squares as desired and work the filet design with beads of your choice.

Necklace Drop Diagram

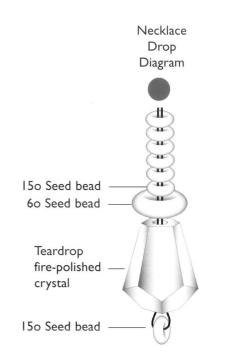

15o Seed bead ———
6o Seed bead ———

Teardrop fire-polished crystal ———

15o Seed bead ———

black lace necklace blank

4

bridal bag

pattern works up into a long
rectangular design that is
joined together to form a
tube, lined with fabric, and
finished with braided cord.
This bag is the embodiment
of the old wedding verse
about something old, something new, and something
blue. It is just the right size
for keeping the day's neces-
sities such as a lipstick or
mints. It also can be used for
collecting mementos and
small gifts such as dollar
bills that are given to the
bride and groom as part of
a tradition enjoyed by many
families all over the world.

materials

> <u>Beads</u>
> 15o Seed beads: Toho 762 matte cream (120 grams)
>
> <u>Other materials</u>
> Braided cord: off-white, 1 yard
> Cardboard, lightweight: 6" square
> Fine-gauge knit fabric, lightweight: cream, ¼ yard
> Leather, lightweight: cream, 6" square
> Polyester batting, lightweight
> Thread: off-white
> White glue

instructions

Note: Toho beads are specifically recommended for this project as they have larger holes than Miyuki in this size.

1 Refer to Filet-beading Primer on pages 32–35. Weave design according to Bridal Bag Chart below and on page 45.

a. Determine the number of patterns (pats) in the bottom, or foundation, row of the design. In the Bridal Bag, there are 96. This design is worked in the round, so the first pat is attached to the last pat on each row. The formula for determining the number of beads required to form the foundation row in a circular pattern is:

(4 x # of pats)

Thus, the number of beads required to form the foundation row of the Bridal Bag is (4 x 96) = 384.

b. Thread on 384 beads.

Note: Put your beads into a low-edged container (such as the plastic disposables available in most supermarkets) and scoop through them several times with the needle. You will pick up several beads. Slip these on the thread.

The 384 15o seed beads will accumulate to a length of at least 15", so there is no need to count until you have

bridal bag chart — left

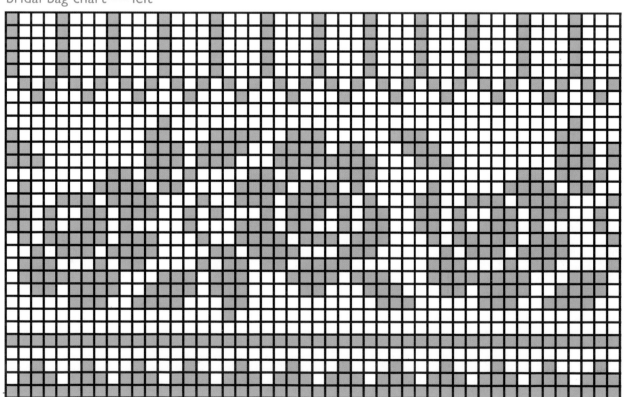

reached a length of at least 12" or more. To mark the count, you can tie a second thread through a bead at the point of your choice as shown in Illustration A. This way you only need to count after that point each time.

Illustration A

beads onto the thread. Skip the first 11 beads on the thread, and run the needle through the 12th bead. Run the needle back through the last three beads in the loop, then take up the slack in the thread at this point. Run the needle through the back of the fourth bead—this will stabilize this bead so it becomes the top bead of the center "leg" of a filled pat. Slip five beads over the needle. Skip one bead on the bottom row, then run the needle through the next bead. Run the needle back through the last three beads on the leg, take up the slack, then run the needle through the back of the fourth bead—this forms the third leg of the filled pat (and the first leg of the next pat).

d. Work in this manner until you have added a total of 95 pats. Work the center leg of the 96th pat, then add only one bead. At this point, lay the foundation row out on a flat surface to make certain that it is not twisted.

c. Work the pats of the foundation row, from right to left: All pats on this row are filled. For the first pat, add nine

e. Join the 96th pat to the first pat by running the needle through three beads on the outside edge of

bridal bag chart — right

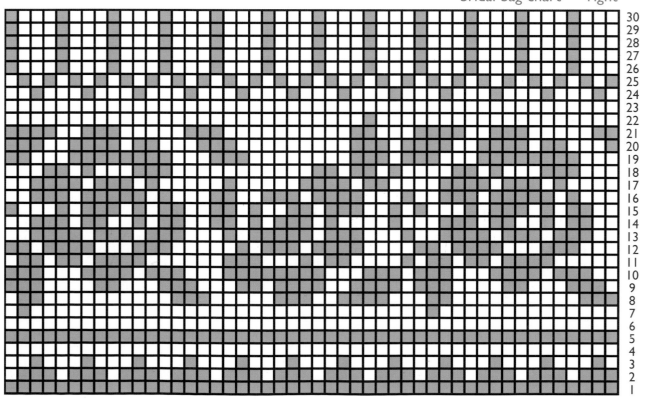

30
29
28
27
26
25
24
23
22
21
20
19
18
17
16
15
14
13
12
11
10
9
8
7
6
5
4
3
2
1

the first pat. Take up the slack, then work the thread through the beads until it emerges in the top bead of any pat leg—this will be your starting point for the second round. Using the extra length of thread left at the end of the original 384-bead strand, attach the bottom of the foundation row. Adjust the tension as needed and bury the excess thread in the beads of the original 384-bead strand, looping as needed until it is secure.

f. The first pat of round two (worked again from right to left on the chart now that the design is in the round) is filled. Add nine beads. Skip the nonleg bead and run the needle through the top bead of the next leg on the first round. Run the needle back through the last three beads, take up the slack, then run the needle through the back of the fourth bead, creating the center leg. Slip five beads over the needle. Skip one bead on the row below, then run the needle through the next bead. Run the needle back through the last three beads on the leg, take up the slack, then run the needle through the back of the fourth bead.

g. When you come to a pat that is open, add seven beads. Skip three beads on the row below and run the needle through the top bead of the next leg on the first round. Run the needle through the last three beads to form the leg of the pat.

h. Continue working the design as charted, repeating the directions for open and filled patterns as previously described.

2 Work the cord channel. Following Illustration B, work this trim as you would a row of filet where open and filled pats alternate, only working each leg so that it is six beads tall instead of three.

Close-up view of filet beading on Bridal Bag.

3 Work the lace. To begin the lace, bring the thread up in the top bead of any center leg of a filled pat in the cord-channel row. [Add 21 beads and run the needle through the top bead of the center leg of the next filled pat, following Illustration C. Run the needle through the last five beads on the loop. *Add 16 beads and run the needle through the top bead of the center leg of the next filled pat, following Illustration D. Run the needle through the last five beads on the loop. * Repeat between *'s until the next to last loop. Add 11 beads, join to the first loop], and bring needle out in the center bead of the first loop, following Illustration E. Repeat between [ ]'s for a second row of loops. Adjust the tension as needed and bury the excess thread in the beads.

Illustration C   Illustration D

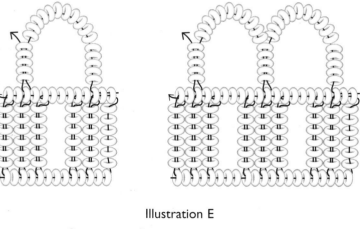

Illustration E

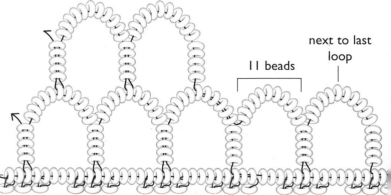

11 beads   next to last loop

4 After completing the weave, place the finished beadwork on a flat surface, and measure its doubled width. Use the resulting measurement to determine the diameter of the base of the purse, using this formula: (width) multiplied by 2, then divided by pi (3.1427). Using 15o beads, the resulting doubled width should be about 8". Thus, 8" x 2 = 16", divided by 3.1427 = 5.09". If you were using 11o beads, the resulting size would be larger. Cut cardboard into a circle of the correct diameter.

5 Using the cardboard as a template, cut a circle of knit fabric ½" larger all around than the cardboard. Notch as shown in Illustration F. Pull the notched excess toward the center of the cardboard and glue in place as shown in Illustration G.

Notes: Use masking tape to secure notches while drying, if necessary. The masking tape will be removed later.

Be certain that the fabric is pulled just enough to bring the cut entirely onto the cardboard so no raw edge will show later.

6 Using the fabric-coated cardboard as a template, cut the leather 1/16" smaller all around. Remove masking tape, then glue the leather in place so it covers all the notches. This will form the underside of the base of the bag.

7 Cut a piece of knit fabric the same size as the filet area of the beadwork. The rough size of the piece for the bag as shown is 16" x 5⅜". Do not include the cord channel or the lace in the measurement. Join the two short sides together with thread and overcast stitches as shown in Illustration H.

8 Slip the seamed knit fabric inside the beadwork; baste the fabric onto the beadwork a few rows below the cord-channel row with thread and long basting stitches as shown in Illustration I.

Note: The basting will be removed later.

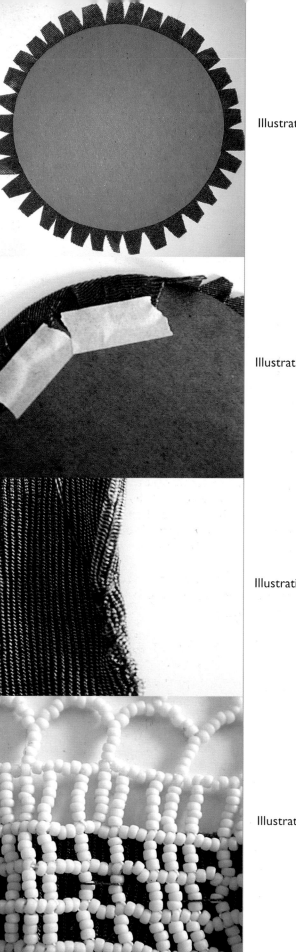

Illustration F

Illustration G

Illustration H

Illustration I

Illustration J   Illustration L

Illustration K   Illustration M

9 Join the knit fabric to the beadwork along the horizontal row just below the cord-channel row, running the needle about ⅛" into the knit and using small stitches, spaced at intervals of every other bead as shown in Illustration J. Do the same along the bottom edge, but space stitches every third bead as shown in Illustration K. Remove basting stitches.

10 Join the bottom edge of the lined bag to the covered cardboard base by pinning the two pieces together as shown in Illustration L, positioning the lined filet evenly around the edge of base. Sew the base onto the lined bag all around with invisible stitches as shown in Illustration M.

11 Weave the braided cord through the slots in the cord-channel row at the top of the bag. Tie the two ends of cord together in a tight knot and trim frayed ends.

filet beading blank   Use this blank to create your own filet beading design.

ladder bead-weaving primer

The beaded ladder is one of the most versatile techniques in beading. Using two needles on opposite ends of the same thread, the basic concept is to create attached "rows" of beads that can be used as a foundation for larger projects. To create ladders, bugle beads and seed beads (including delicas) can be used alone or combined with different bead types.

weaving a basic ladder

Illustration A

Cut a length of thread that is approximately 36". Place one needle on each end. Slip one bugle bead onto the thread to the center of its length. Slip another bugle bead onto either end of the thread, then insert the remaining needle into the opposite end of the

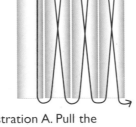

bugle bead as shown in Illustration A. Pull the thread ends taut. Continue adding bugle beads in this manner until your ladder is the desired length. Proceed with the design following the project instructions.

variations on a ladder

This section provides four very different projects—each starting with a ladder foundation. The Bridal Necklace on page 51 demonstrates how to string seed beads and fire-polished crystals across one side of the ladder. The Bugle Earrings on page 54 show how to join a simple ladder into a tube by wrapping it around a paper core. The Pyramids Bracelet on page 56 starts with a simple ladder but soon develops peaks by stacking six bugles every three beads on the ladder. Finally, the Rainbow Bracelet on page 58 demonstrates how to combine the ladder with bead stringing as it requires looping a number of seed beads in and out of the bugles.

bridal necklace

an elegant piece need not be difficult to work or take a long time to complete. This sparkling white necklace is quite simple to make and takes less than three hours. The ladder is created using #5 bugles (roughly ½" long) and embellished with crystals. It is the perfect "something new" accessory for the bride to wear as she walks down the aisle— all attention focused on her and her beautiful wedding ensemble.

materials

Beads
#5 Bugle beads, matte crystal (172)
6mm Fire-polished crystals, milk white AB (57)
15o Seed beads, Miyuki 470 crystal AB (2 grams)
11o Seed beads, Toho 169F matte crystal AB (4 grams)

Other materials
Thread, lightweight nylon: white
White glue

instructions

Note: Because bugle beads often have sharp edges, it is important to create the initial ladder using a thread that will stand up to the edges. When the ladder is complete, you can tie on lighter-weight thread to complete the design. Take care with your thread tension when creating the ladder; avoid pulling it so tight that it puckers, but be certain to keep an eye on the thread slack so the bugles lay neatly next to each other. When new threads are needed, tie them on with a square knot.

1 Refer to Ladder Bead-weaving Primer on page 50. Create the ladder.

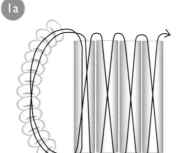

a. Cut a 36" length of thread and place one needle on each end. String 13 11o seed beads and one bugle onto the thread. Form a loop; run the thread through it twice for strength. The threads should emerge from both sides of the bugle bead.

b. Continue adding bugle beads with both threads to create a ladder until there are 172 bugles in the ladder.

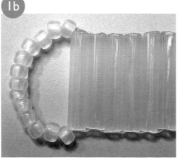

2 Add 11o seed beads onto the sides of the ladder.

a. Set one of the threads aside (the dormant thread) and use the other (active thread) to attach 11o seed beads. The thread should emerge from one side of the bugle bead next to the loop. Set this thread aside.

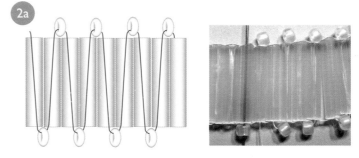

b. Pick up the previously dormant thread so that it is now the active one. Add 11o seed beads onto the sides. The thread should emerge from the other side of the bugle bead nearest the loop.

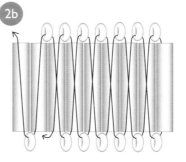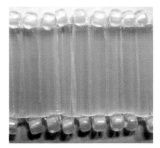

3 Add crystal crisscrosses.

a. Add four 15o seed beads, one crystal, and four more 15o seed beads. Then skip two bugles on the ladder and take the thread through the opposite side of the third bugle bead. Continue in this manner for the entire length of the ladder until the active thread emerges from the last bugle bead.

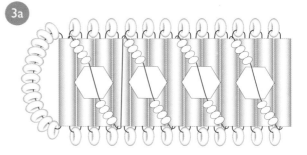

b. Pick up the other thread and add four 15o seed beads, then run the needle through the crystal on the first leg of the crisscross. Add four 15o seed beads, skip two bugles on the ladder and take the thread through the opposite side of the third bugle bead. Continue in this manner until the thread emerges from the last bugle on the ladder.

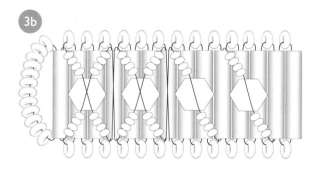

3b

4 Create the clasp.

a. Add five 15o seed beads, one crystal, then one 11o seed bead. Skip the 11o seed bead and run the thread back through the crystal, then add five more 15o seed beads. Run the thread through the last bugle bead. Reinforce with the same action, using the other thread.

b. Weave the threads through the bugle ladder until they emerge from the same side of the bracelet. Tie a knot close to the ladder, add a dab of glue to the knot and ½" of the excess thread. Bury the thread in the next bugle bead and trim. Wipe off excess glue before it dries.

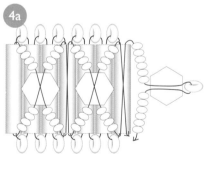

4a

4b

The Peridot Bracelet is worked using the same technique as the Bridal Necklace. The ladder was simply shortened to fit around the wrist and the bead colors were changed to gold, green, and blue.

bugle earrings

quick to make, these charming earrings are formed from a short ladder that is made up of #5 bugle beads. The completed ladder is wrapped around a paper core and finished with shiny silver jewelry components. Change the color of the bugles and the finish of the components to match your particular needs. To create a different look, try using satin bugle beads with cat's eye beads as the embellishment.

instructions

1 Refer to Ladder Bead-weaving Primer on page 50. Create a ladder of bugle beads approximately 1⅛" long, using two needles.

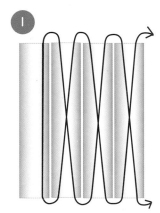

materials

Beads
#5 Bugle beads, matte light blue (60)
11o Seed bead, matte light blue (4)

Other materials
Bead caps, 12 mm diameter, silver (4)
Ear wires, silver (2)
Head pins, 1½" (2)
Paper strips for paper tubes, as wide as the bugles
   are long, approximately 10" in length
Thread, lightweight: white

2 Form a paper tube about ⅜" diameter. The width of the tube should be the same as the length of the bugle beads.

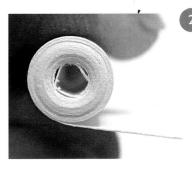

3 Wrap the ladder around the paper tube; add a bugle bead if needed for fit. Join the first and last bugle beads together, then bury the thread within the ladder and trim. Slip the paper tube partway out of the ladder round and run a thin line of glue all around the edge of the paper tube. Slide the ladder round back in place. Assemble on a head pin as shown

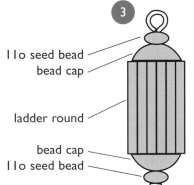

11o seed bead
bead cap

ladder round

bead cap
11o seed bead

4 After assembly, trim the head pin to ⅜" and turn into a loop. Attach the loop to the ear wire and close the loop.

pyramids bracelet

stunning in its simplicity, this piece is striking in its appearance. It is created by stringing together a ladder of #5 bugle beads and strategically stacking six more at a time to create the peaks, or pyramids. Contrasting seed beads are incorporated into the design to give the bugles a finished edge. This bracelet can be made to any length desired as long as you follow the instructions required to maintain the pattern. If it were made quite a bit longer, the design could become a glitzy strap on an evening bag.

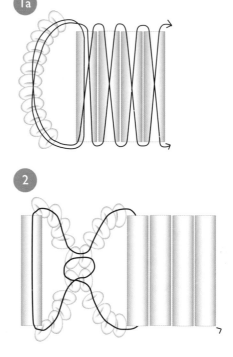

materials

Beads
#5 Bugle beads, silver-lined gold (155)
15o Seed beads, matte dark blue (308)
11o Seed beads, silver-lined gold (32)

Other materials
Thread, lightweight nylon: tan

instructions

1 Refer to Ladder Bead-weaving Primer on page 50. Create the ladder.

a. Cut a 36" length of thread and place one needle on each end. String 12 11o seed beads and one bugle onto the thread as shown. Form the toggle loop end; run the thread through it twice for strength. The threads should emerge from both sides of the bugle bead.

b. Continue adding bugle beads with both threads to create a ladder until there are 76 bugles in the ladder.

Note: The length should be a multiple of seven plus six to form the pattern correctly.

2 Add the toggle end of the bracelet by stringing on 20 11o seed beads and one bugle as shown. Reinforce with a second round of threading as on the loop end.

3 Work the thread back through the toggle and ladder until it emerges from the last bugle of the ladder.

4 Create the pyramids on the ladder.

a. Stack bugle beads on the ladder in a pyramid pattern as shown and weave them into place.

b. When the bugle pyramid is complete, go back and add the 15o seed beads at each end of each bugle bead.

c. Skip three bugles on the ladder, work the next pyramid, then the 15o seed beads at the ends.

d. Continue in this manner until you reach the end of the bracelet.

5 Bury the excess thread within the weave and clip it when it is secure.

rainbow bracelet

a high degree of color and texture are achieved in this lively bracelet. It begins with sparkling silver-lined bugle beads strung in a ladder and continues with matte seed beads of varying sizes that loop above and below the ladder, linking together the repeating colors of the rainbow. This design provides an easy-to-make, fun-to-wear piece of jewelry that can be added to your own collection or given away to someone who will love wearing it as much as you do.

bead code

#2 Czech bugle beads (1 for every ½" of ladder):
   silver-lined gold

   silver-lined lime

   silver-lined medium blue-green

   silver-lined aqua

   silver-lined sapphire

   silver-lined lavender

15o Seed beads:
   Miyuki 132FR matte topaz AB (13 for every ½" of ladder plus 24)

Delica beads:
   Miyuki 860 matte lime (12 for every ½" of ladder)

11o Seed beads:
   matte opaque medium green (12 for every ½" of ladder)

   matte opaque aqua (12 for every ½" of ladder)

8o Seed beads:
   opaque light sapphire (8 for every ½" of ladder)

6o Seed beads:
   matte opaque light lavender (6 for every ½" of ladder)

6mm Glass beads:
   opaque light blue (2)

materials

Beads as listed in bead code
Thread, medium-weight: white
White glue

instructions

1 Refer to Ladder Bead-weaving Primer on page 50.

2 Cut a length of thread that is approximately 36". Place a needle on both ends of the thread. Create a ladder of bugle beads that is slightly larger than the size of your wrist with an odd number of repeats. Start with a gold bugle, then add lavender, sapphire, aqua, medium blue-green, and lime bugles in a repeat pattern. After the last repeat, add one more gold bugle to the ladder. The thread ends should each emerge from a gold bugle.

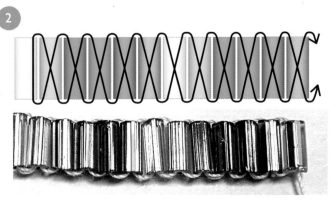

3 Drop one thread; the other thread becomes the active thread. Add loops.

a. Add 13 matte topaz 15o seed beads, then run the thread through the next gold bugle on the ladder. Continue in this fashion until the thread is run through the next-to-the-last gold bugle on the ladder.

b. Run the thread through the next lime bugle in the opposite direction; add 12 matte lime delica beads. Going back in the opposite direction, run the thread through the next lime bugle on the ladder. Repeat until the thread emerges from the last lime bugle.

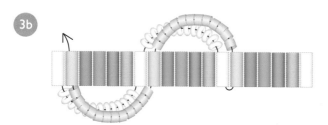

c. Run the thread in the opposite direction through the first medium blue-green bugle. Add 12 matte opaque medium green 11o seed beads; run the thread through the next medium blue-green bugle on the ladder. Repeat until you reach the last medium blue-green bugle on the ladder.

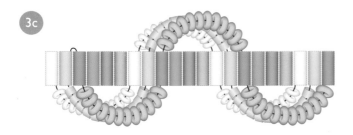

d. Run the thread in the opposite direction through the last aqua bugle. Add 12 matte opaque aqua 11o seed beads; run the thread through the next aqua bugle on the ladder. Repeat until you run the thread through the first aqua bugle on the ladder.

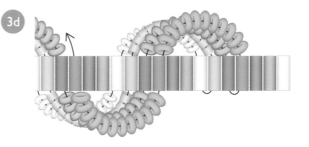

e. Run the thread in the opposite direction through the first sapphire bugle. Add eight opaque light sapphire 8o seed beads. Run the thread through the next sapphire bugle. Repeat until you run the thread through the last sapphire bugle.

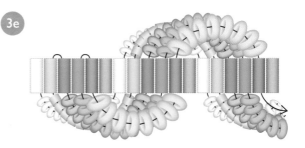

f. Run the thread in the opposite direction through the last lavender bugle. Add six opaque light lavender 6o seed beads. Run the thread through the next lavender bugle. Repeat until the thread emerges from the first lavender bugle.

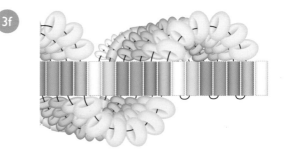

4 Create the clasp.

a. On the left side (beginning) of the bracelet, add 13 matte topaz 15o seed beads. Run the needle back through the first gold bugle on the ladder. Add one 6mm glass bead and one 15o matte topaz bead. Run the thread back through the light blue glass bead. Repeat this to fortify the clasp.

Note: The bead clasp works by inserting the glass bead into the loop on the opposite end of the bracelet as shown in Illustration A.

alternate designs

Try using a single color to create this bracelet. In the photo below, ivory beads were used to create a more traditional-looking piece. If you would like to make a necklace using this design, create a ladder that is 16" long. Work the bead loops as previously described.

b. Run the thread back through all the matte topaz 15o beads and gold bugles in a continuous run, until the thread emerges from the next-to-the-last gold bugle on the ladder. Add 12 matte topaz 15o beads. Run the needle back through the last gold bugle on the ladder. Add the remaining 6mm glass bead and one 15o matte topaz bead. Run the thread back through the last gold bugle. Repeat this to fortify the clasp.

5 Weave the excess thread into the bracelet; apply a dot of glue to the thread, then weave through one last time. Wipe off excess glue and trim the thread.

6 Return to the previous clasp end and pick up the dormant thread. Reinforce the clasp end with the dormant thread, then bury the excess as described in Step 5.

loom bead-weaving primer

Loom bead-weaving is one of the most elegant methods of beading. Designs are worked from charts in horizontal rows, so color placement is precise and accurate. Seed beads are the most frequent choice in weaving, but square beads and bugles can also be used, depending on the pattern. For the designs in this book, delica beads were selected.

There is something very magical and inspiring about a loom that is warped and ready for beads—it evokes all kinds of possibilities.

looms

Looms can be very helpful in weaving large (or long) pieces that might otherwise be cumbersome to handle. Looms are available in a wonderful assortment of sizes, from tiny tabletop dime-store models to standing giants that can be used for foot-wide, yard-long creations that will take your breath away.

Choose a loom that suits your own preferences. Before buying a loom, decide how wide you'd like to be able to weave, because the width of what you can weave will be limited by the usable width of the loom.

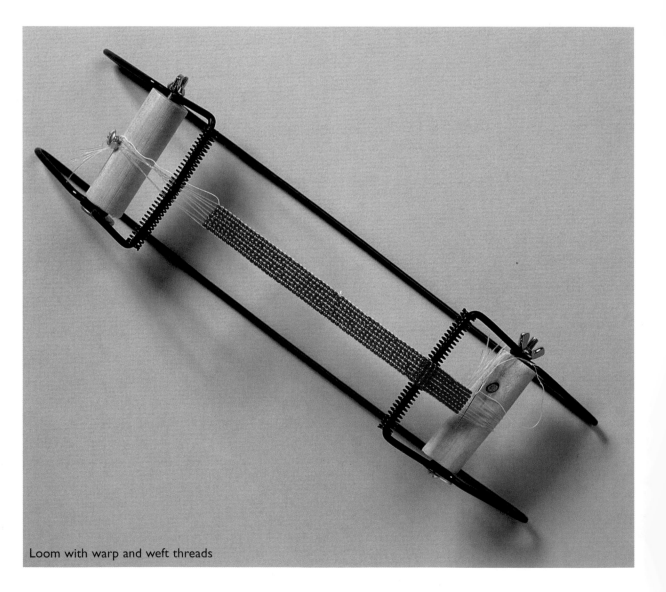

Loom with warp and weft threads

Most of the patterns in this book were woven on a medium-sized standing loom that allows the weaver to roll the ongoing work so the length of the finished piece can exceed the height of the loom itself; the maximum width is roughly 9".

warp and weft

Before you begin weaving, the loom must be strung with vertical threads (warp). Warp the loom according to the instructions provided with your loom. If you plan to incorporate the warp threads into the finishing of the piece, for example, as part of tied fringe, use a thread that will blend into the fringing material. Medium-weight nylon threads are suitable for use as warp.

The basic technique behind loom bead-weaving is to anchor beads in a specific order or pattern onto vertical (warp) threads by passing the horizontal thread (weft) through the row of beads twice, once behind the warp threads and once in front of the warp threads.

weaving the design

Following manufacturer's instructions, warp the loom with the required number of warp threads. This number is figured by counting the number of beads across the width of the design and adding one more.

Cut one 30" length of thread and thread the needle. To start the horizontal (or weft) thread, knot the end of the thread onto the left outermost warp thread as shown in Illustration A. You will be working the design from left to right, top to bottom.

Following the design chart, slip the beads for the top horizontal row onto the needle.

Illustration A

Pass the beaded thread under warp threads, positioning the beads and threads so one bead falls between two warp threads.

After the beads are seated into the warp, pass the needle back through the beads so the weft thread goes over the warp threads.

Repeat for remaining horizontal rows.

To work decreases, pass the weft thread under the outermost warp thread and back through one or more beads on the previous row as required to arrive at the warp thread where the next row begins as shown in Illustration B. Wrap the weft thread around this warp thread and begin the next row.

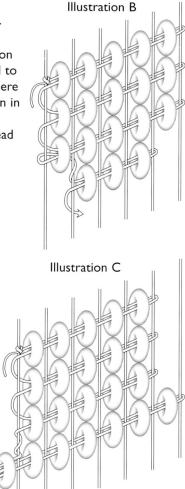

Illustration B

To work increases, wrap the weft thread around the warp thread after completing the previous row as shown in Illustration C. Slip one or more beads as charted (working from within the design toward the left) onto the weft thread, pass the beads under the warp threads, seat them into position, and pass the needle back through the beads so the weft thread goes over the warp threads. Beginning at the point of the increase, slip remaining beads for this row onto the weft thread and proceed as usual.

Illustration C

When the design is complete, bury any excess weft thread in the weave as shown in Illustration D.

Refer to manufacturer's instructions for removing the design from the loom and finishing the warp threads. Refer also to the project instructions for finishing warp threads.

Illustration D

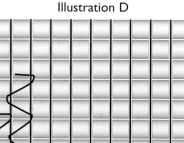

kilim rug

when designing a beaded piece, be aware of the patterns around you wherever you go. This design was inspired by a colorful Kilim rug. The original was handwoven in wool, with predominantly red coloration. Choose colors that complement each other on the color wheel and evoke emotions that you would like to communicate in your piece. Try substituting bead colors and weaving this design in shades of gray accented by black and red to accomplish a completely differently mood.

bead code

 Delica beads:
    matte cream (2946)

 matte light topaz AB (774)

 opaque dyed pumpkin (414)

 matte opaque rose (2498)

 opaque medium lavender (656)

 opaque dark blue (1320)

 matte opaque seafoam (3438)

 matte metallic medium green AB (336)

matte opaque bright turquoise (858)

matte metallic medium olive (548)

opaque medium blue (594)

materials

Beads as listed in bead code
Loom: large enough to accommodate
    a 5½" x 9½" weave
Thread, lightweight: white

instructions

1 Refer to Loom Bead-weaving Primer on pages 62–63. Warp
   the loom with 103 threads to accommodate a design width
   of 102 beads.

2 Work the design according to Kilim Rug Chart on pages
   66–69 in horizontal rows from the top down.

3 When removing the piece from the loom, leave the warp
   threads as long as possible, as they will be incorporated
   in the fringe.

4 Smooth the finished piece to eliminate puckers and gaps.

5 Create a fringe on both the top and bottom edges of
   the piece:

a. Starting at the bottom
left, run a single thread
through each of the first
three consecutive beads.

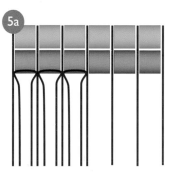

b. Gather these 10 threads
and tie them together into
a knot.

c. Run a single thread
through each of the next
three consecutive beads.
Gather nine threads from
these beads and tie them
together into a knot.
Continue in this manner.

d. Push each knot as close
to the weave as possible.

e. When all the fringes are
tied, cut them to the same
length.

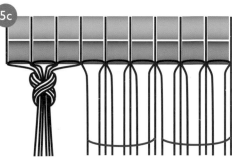

kilim rug chart — top left

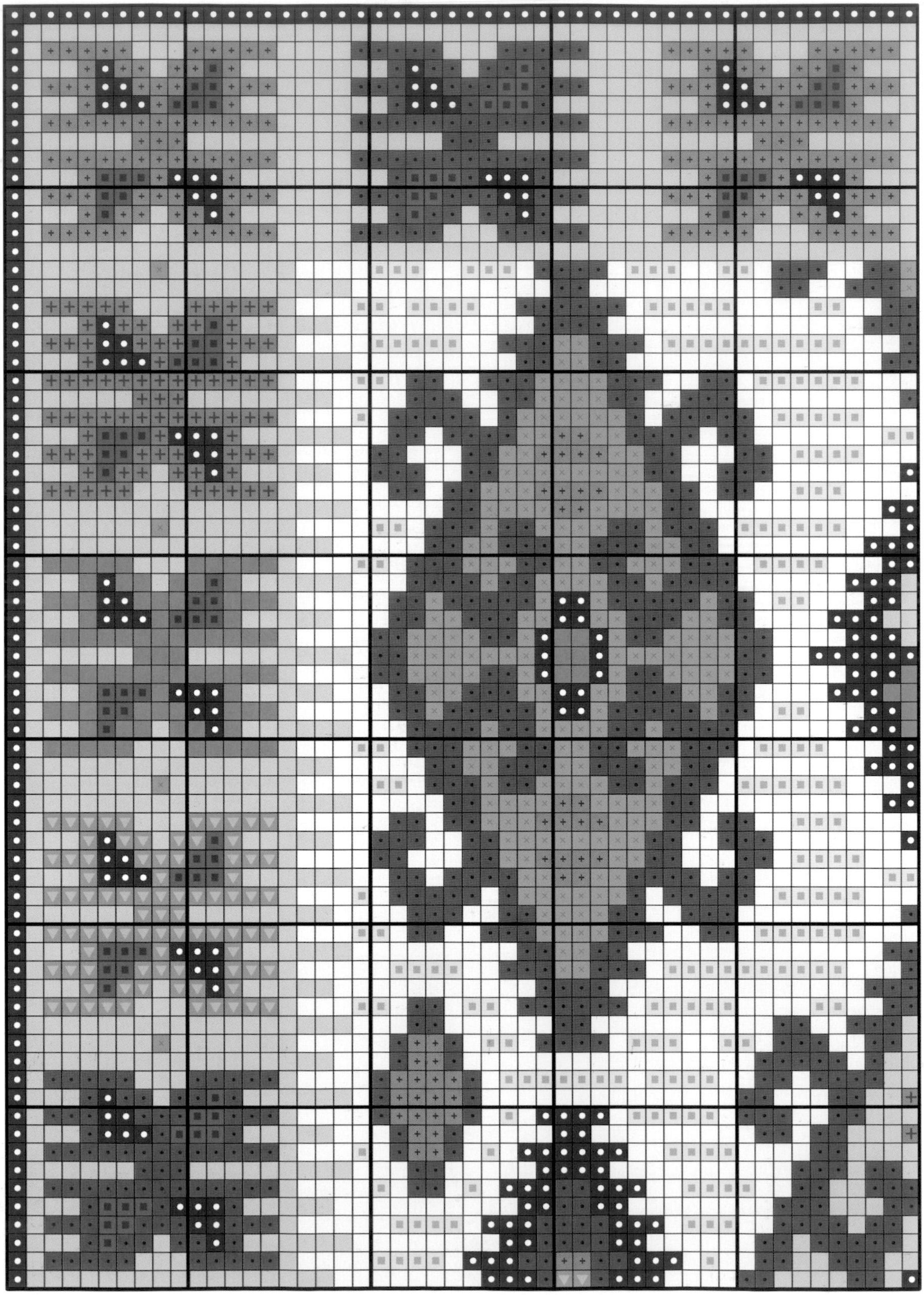

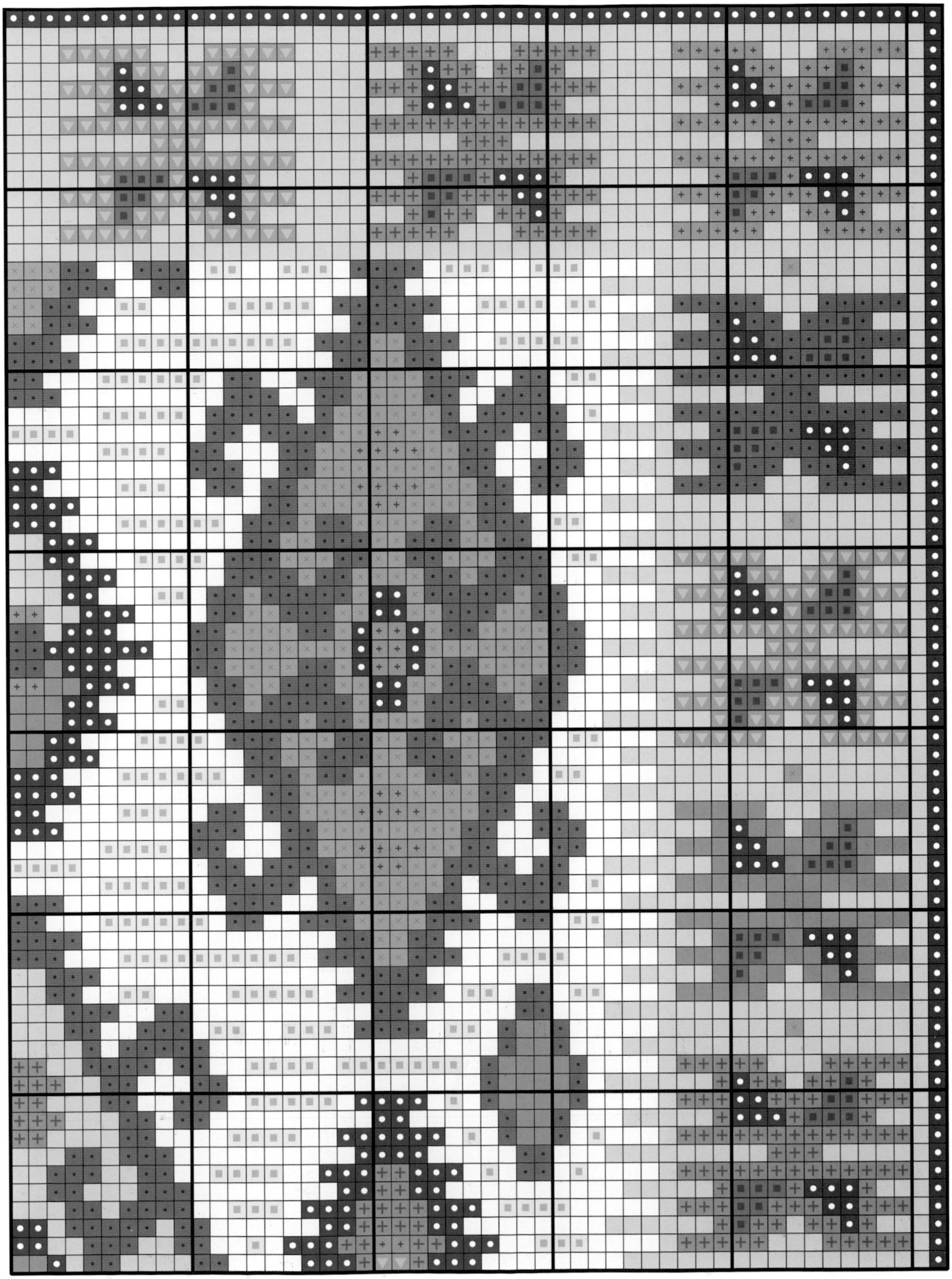

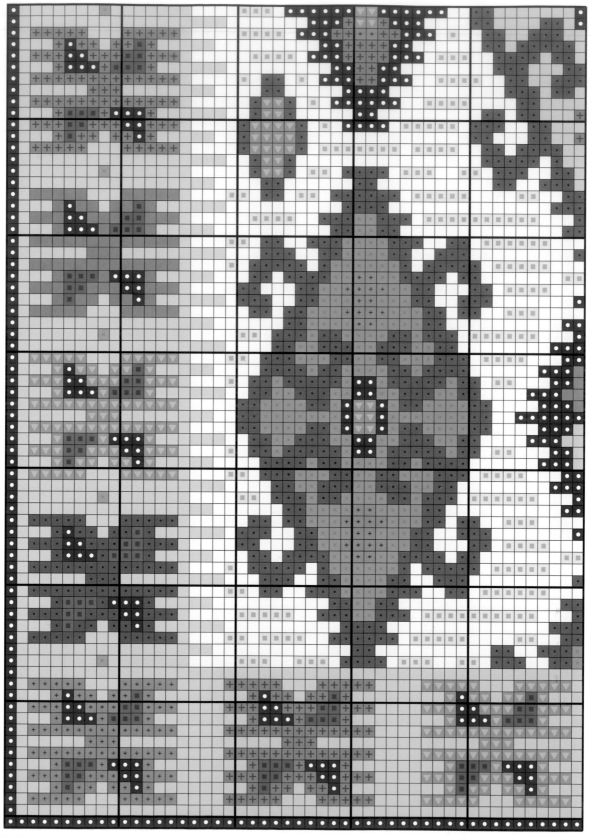

kilim rug chart — bottom left

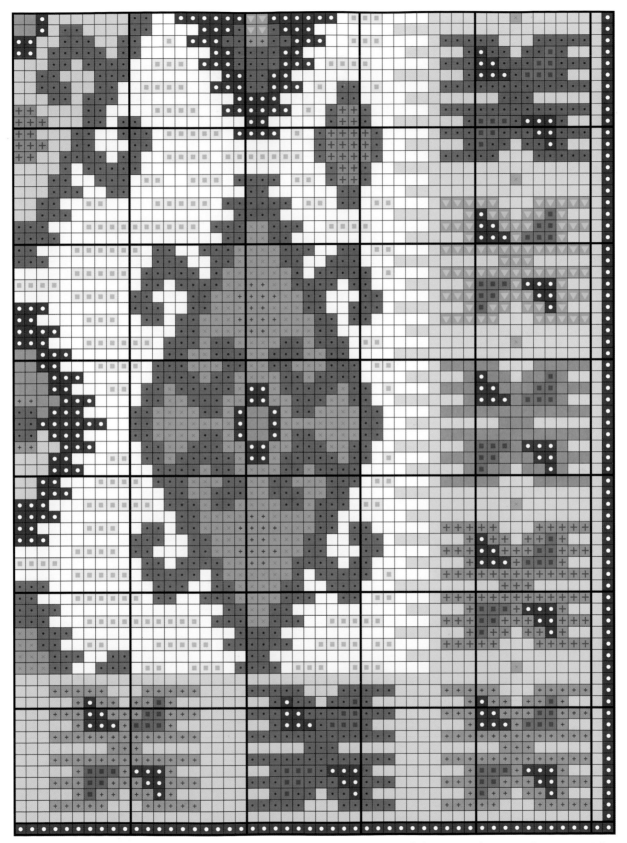

camellias

nature has encouraged artists for centuries. This piece was inspired by a Ming Dynasty tapestry held in the National Collection of the People's Republic of China. The original piece had a solid neutral background; whereas, in this design, the bird and flowered branches are placed on a backdrop that resembles a lovely summer sunset. The piece is finished by tying the warp threads together to create a fringe.

materials

Beads as listed in bead code
Loom: large enough to accommodate
  an 8" x 11" weave
Thread, lightweight: off-white

instructions

1 Refer to Loom Bead-weaving Primer on pages 62–63. Warp the loom with 103 threads to accommodate a design width of 102 beads.

2 Work the design according to Camellias Chart on pages 72–75 in horizontal rows from the top down.

3 Refer to Kilim Rug on pages 64–65 and repeat Steps 3–5 to fringe threads.

bead code

 Delica beads:
  Miyuki 353 matte cream (2055)

 Miyuki 1363 opaque dyed salmon (378)

Miyuki 1371 opaque dyed rose (383)

Miyuki 800 matte opaque dusty rose (372)

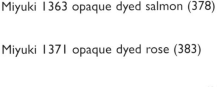 Miyuki 1376 opaque dyed dark rose (479)

Miyuki 356 matte lavender (440)

 Miyuki 379 matte taupe-lavender (442)

 Miyuki 799 matte opaque purple (262)

 Miyuki 771 matte transparent gold (24)

 Miyuki 371 matte light olive (198)

Miyuki 657 opaque tobacco (246)

Miyuki 877 matte opaque light green (272)

 Miyuki 655 opaque medium green (307)

Miyuki 656 opaque dark green (210)

Miyuki 653 opaque dyed pumpkin (65)

Miyuki 794 matte opaque chestnut (104)

Miyuki 734 opaque dark brown (274)

Miyuki 798 matte denim blue (80)

Miyuki 659 opaque medium blue (181)

Miyuki 879 matte opaque light blue (180)

camellias chart — top left

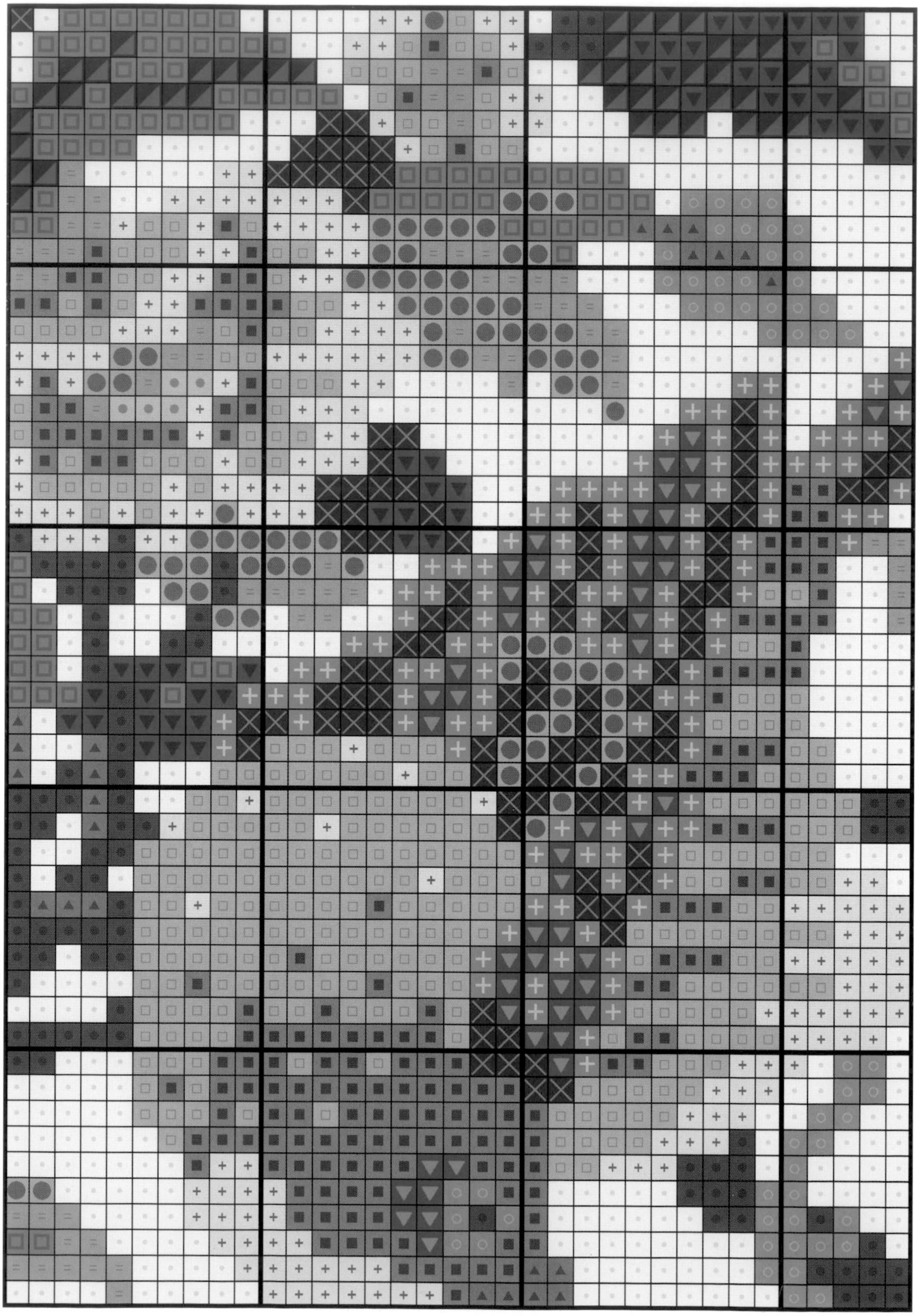

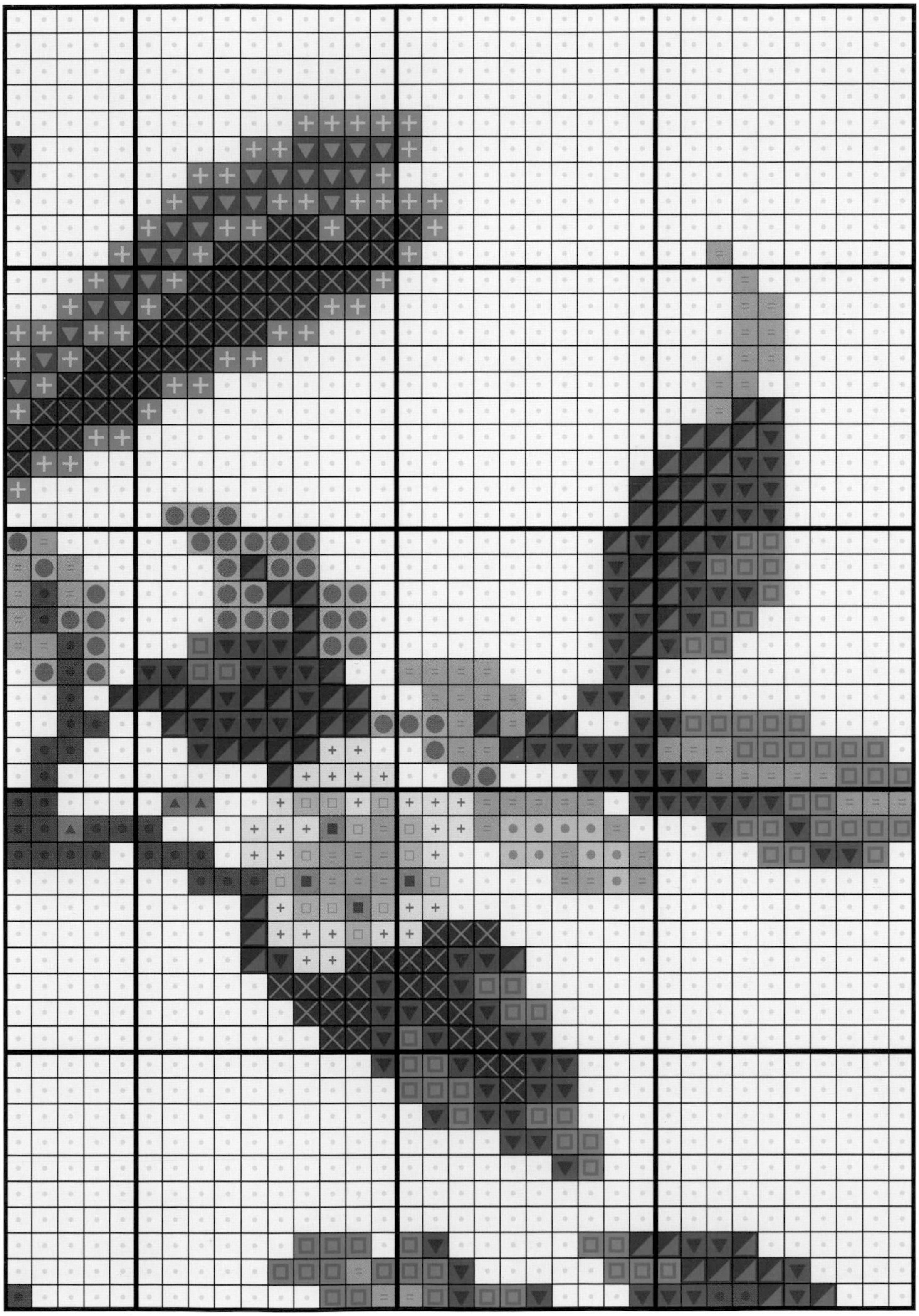

camellias chart — bottom left

camellias chart — bottom right

garden sunset

shaped pieces

can be created on a loom by weaving increases and decreases into the design. The point on the bottom of this piece is finished with a beaded drop. A dowel is inserted at the top to stabilize the bead-work and a hanger is added so you can display this botanical beauty. This Victorian-flavored bouquet of flowers will remain a joy to you long after the blooms cut from your garden have faded and withered away.

bead code

 Delica beads:
Miyuki 42 silver-lined gold (921)

 Miyuki 203 lustered cream (536)

 Miyuki 233 Ceylon yellow (309)

 Miyuki 67 lined light salmon (418)

 Miyuki 855 matte persimmon (456)

 Miyuki 355 matte metallic lavender-pink (219)

 Miyuki 255 lined light pink (257)

 Miyuki 245 lined rose (174)

 Miyuki 75 lined red (208)

 Miyuki 796 matte dark red (183)

 Miyuki 663 opaque dark olive (198)

 Miyuki 237 Ceylon light green (332)

 Miyuki 877 matte medium green AB (456)

 Miyuki 859 matte emerald AB (424)

 Miyuki 1479 opaque dyed pumpkin (99)

 Miyuki 755 matte opaque light blue (155)

 Miyuki 659 opaque medium blue (125)

 Miyuki 798 matte dark denim blue (50)

 4mm Round crystals, topaz (3)

 6mm Round crystals, topaz (2)

10mm Round crystal, topaz (1)

6–8mm Flat disks with horizontal hole, aventurine, (2)

4mm Square bead, galvanized gold (1)

materials

Beads as listed in bead code
Loom: large enough to accommodate
  an 8" x 11" weave
Thread, lightweight: off-white
White glue
Wooden dowel, ¼" diameter: 2¾"
  long with smoothed edges

instructions

1 Refer to Loom Bead-weaving Primer on pages 62–63. Warp the loom with 50 threads to accommodate a design width of 49 beads. When you attach the weft thread, leave a tail of at least 8", which will be used later in the finishing.

2 Work the design according to Garden Sunset Chart on pages 78–79 as follows:

a. Begin at the top of the pattern and weave downward. Decrease at the base of the design to achieve the V shape.

3 When removing the piece from the loom, leave warp threads as long as possible, as they will be used in the finishing.

4 Smooth the finished piece to eliminate puckers and gaps.

5 Finish the top:

a. Apply a line of glue to the dowel, then position the top warp threads in the glue, leaving a space of about 1" between the dowel and the beads. Carefully wipe off excess glue and allow to dry.

b. Trim off the excess thread, then roll the dowel into the beadwork so it is completely wrapped within the silver-lined gold section at the top.

c. Using the leftover first weft thread, tack the edge of the piece to the body so the tube remains closed. Bury the excess thread within the tube and trim.

6 Create the hanger:

a. Cut a thread length of at least 24". Secure the thread within the tube at the back side of the work then bring it out at the top center.

b. Secure the flat disk at the edge of the beadwork so it lays against and conceals the dowel. Bring the thread out in the base of the flat disk; add four silver-lined gold delicas, one 6mm topaz crystal, and one more silver-lined gold delica. Skipping the last delica, run the thread back through all the beads until it emerges from the top of the flat disk. Add one 4mm topaz crystal, run the thread under the top of the weave on the dowel, and bring it out along the top ridge, seven beads from the side edge. Add 90 silver-lined gold delicas to the thread, then re-insert it into the same row of the weave on the other side, seven beads away from the edge. Bring it out into position and add the decorative beads, working in reverse order from opposite end of hanger.

c. If you have used a thread with good strength, you can bury the thread at this point and trim it. If not, run the thread through the full length of the hanger again, then bury and trim the excess.

7 Finish the bottom:

a. Smooth out the weave of the beadwork, then bury all the excess warp threads within the weave, except the two center threads.

b. To one of the remaining threads, add three silver-lined gold delicas, one 4mm topaz crystal, the square bead, the 10mm topaz crystal, and one delica. Skipping the last delica, run the thread back through all the beads, then bury the excess thread in the weave. Repeat with the other thread for reinforcement.

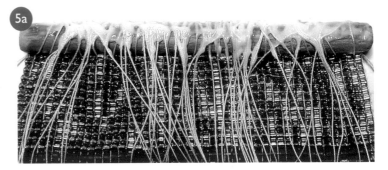

5a

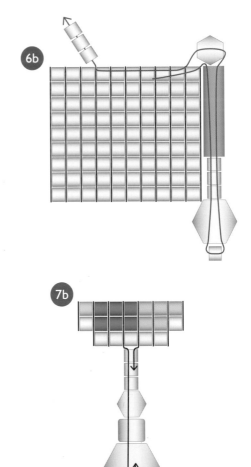

6b

7b

garden sunset chart — top

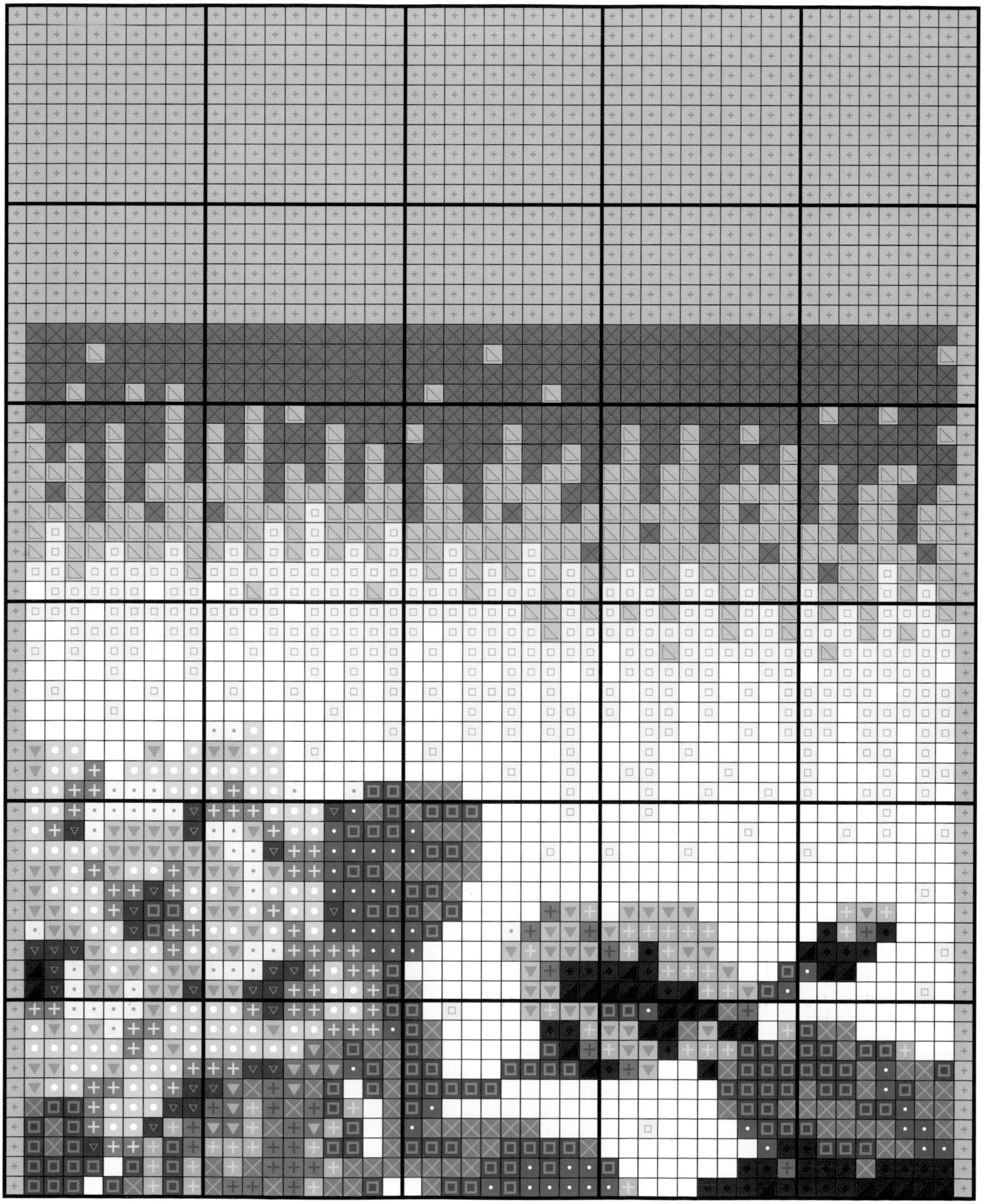

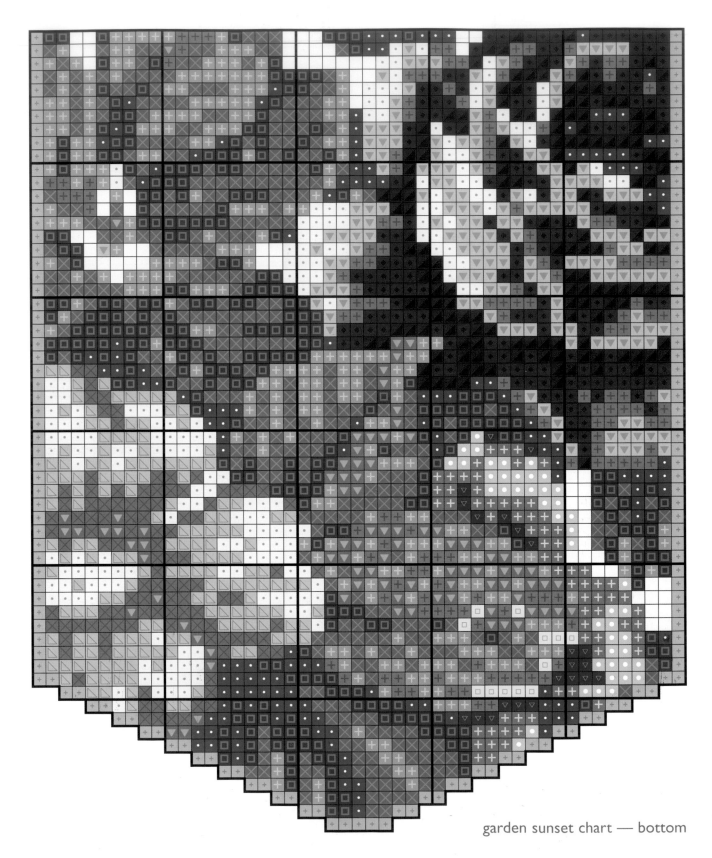

garden sunset chart — bottom

asian designs are known for their disciplined use of color and precise placement of patterns and symbols. Working the design is supposed to bring a person to new levels of understanding how the individual pieces are interdependent upon one another to create a finished piece that is in harmony with itself and the world around it. This piece employs a vibrant color scheme and blends floral designs with geometric symbols in the shape of a hanging kimono. Actual kimonos that are decorated in such a fashion are reserved for dignitaries or for use on very special occasions.

bead code

  Delica beads:

Miyuki 852 matte light topaz AB (954)

Miyuki 651 opaque dyed gold (652)

Miyuki 653 opaque dyed pumpkin (334)

Miyuki 354 matte pale rose (624)

Miyuki 758 matte medium lavender (552)

Miyuki 799 matte opaque purple (150)

Miyuki 371 matte metallic light olive (1700)

Miyuki 324 matte metallic medium green (1179)

Miyuki 22 metallic bronze (5026)

 Miyuki 879 matte opaque light blue (580)

 Miyuki 793 matte aqua (1381)

materials

Beads as listed in bead code
Large decorative beads
Loom: large enough to accommodate
    an 8" x 11" weave
Thread, lightweight: off-white
Wooden dowel, ¼" diameter, 10" long

instructions

1 Refer to Loom Bead-weaving Primer on pages 62–63. Warp
the loom with 136 threads to accommodate a
design width of 135 beads.

2 Work the design according to Kimono Chart on pages
84–86 as follows:

a. Starting from the left side, begin with the top row of the
sleeve section. Start the weave approximately 3½" below
the workable top of the loom. Weave downward in horizontal rows, working decreases from right and left sides,
until the sleeves are complete.

b. Attach a thread where the collar begins, then weave
upward in horizontal rows.

c. Using a pencil to isolate the six warp threads you
will be working with, add the hanging straps that come
off the collar. Attach a thread at the appropriate starting point and weave upward. Weave all the remaining
straps as charted.

d. Refer to Kimono Chart Placement on page 87.
Weave the lower body section of the kimono. Attach
a thread at the point where the body drops down
from the sleeves and weave in horizontal rows to the
bottom as shown on the chart.

3 Remove the woven piece from the loom. Weave the
excess threads back into the beads, except the four
centermost threads at the bottom of the piece.

4 Smooth the finished piece to eliminate any puckers
and gaps in the weave.

5 Fold the straps back so they are all even in height at
the top; sew loops with invisible stitches onto the
backs of the straps.

6 Insert dowel through the loops; attach a decorative
hanger at the ends of the dowel.

7 Using the unwoven warp threads at the bottom center, attach decorative beads such as those shown in
the photo on page 81. Run the thread back through
all but the last bead and bury the excess in the weave.
Trim carefully.

*Note: The large decorative polymer clay bead was created
by Ann Dillon.*

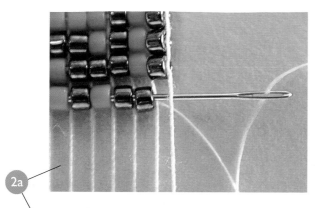

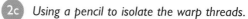

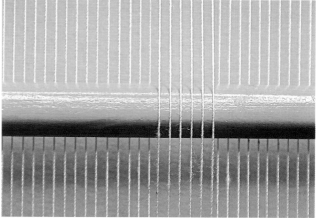

2c *Using a pencil to isolate the warp threads.*

Working decreases from the right.

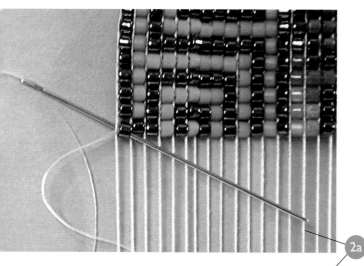

Working decreases from the left.

7 *Burying the excess warp threads in the weave.*

begin here

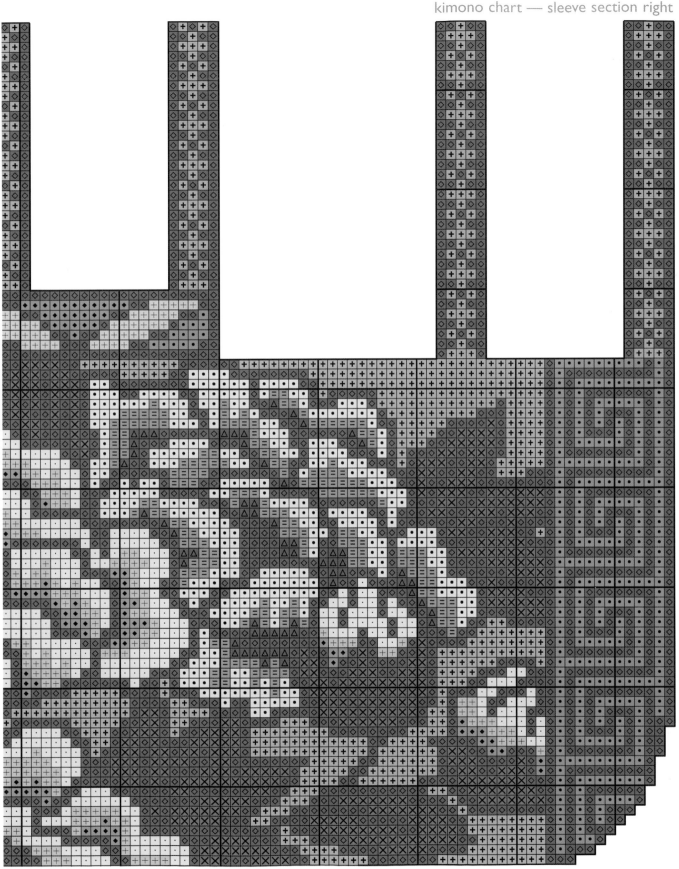

kimono chart — lower body section

needle-weaving primer

Two popular methods of needle-weaving are the brick stitch and the peyote stitch. Seed beads, delica beads, and hex beads are widely used with these two methods. Choose needles and thread that work with the type of bead you are using. A lightweight nylon thread will work well with almost any seed bead. Short ballpoint beading needles in size 10 or 12 are a better choice than longer beading needles.

The charts provided for brick stitch needle-weaving and peyote stitch needle-weaving are drawn to show staggered rows of beads that create a diagonal effect when the design is woven. One gridded oval represents one bead to be worked into the design.

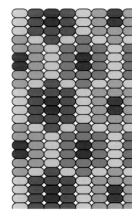 

Brick stitch needle-weaving chart

Peyote stitch needle-weaving chart

Each colored oval found on the chart corresponds to a specific size and color of bead, identified on the bead code which accompanies the chart.

The brick stitch causes beads to lie against one another horizontally while the peyote stitch causes beads to lie vertically against one another.

For each weaving technique, the rows are initially somewhat unstable and may seem difficult to work. Be patient! After two or three rows, the weaving will be quite easy to handle.

brick stitch

Brick stitch is a non-loom weaving technique that creates a strong diagonal weave similar to peyote stitch. It is an excellent choice for small jewelry or accessory pieces where moderate rigidity is required. Designs are worked from charts in horizontal rows and may be shaped by increasing or decreasing.

Note: The diagrams shown here are exaggerated for clarity. When working brick stitch, keep the tension even and consistent; take up the slack in the thread after adding each bead. Avoid pulling too tightly, or the weave may pucker.

Brick stitch always starts with a foundation row. It consists of beads joined side-to-side by thread. You can use either the double-needle technique (top) or the single-needle technique (bottom). In the single-needle method, turn the foundation row so the thread emerges from the bottom of the bead in preparation for starting the second row.

double-needle foundation row

single-needle foundation row

After working the double-needle foundation row, you will let one thread lie dormant while you work rows with the other. Beads are applied individually, looped into the thread between beads on the previous row. Work rows back and forth as charted, increasing or decreasing as required. The top edge of the piece will appear smooth, while the side edges will appear jagged.

asymmetrical brick stitch

Asymmetrical patterns are often used when one end of the pattern will be joined to another, such as in the "beaded bead" shown here. If your pattern is asymmetrical, add rows as shown below, adding an extra bead as you come to the end of each row. Notice in the top and center diagrams that when the last bead is applied, an additional loop of thread is made. This is recommended as it will help to stabilize the ends of the rows.

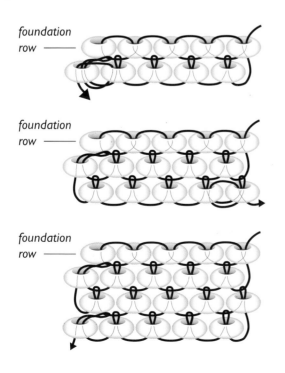

foundation row ———

foundation row ———

foundation row ———

symmetrical brick stitch

Symmetrical brick stitch as shown here is more often used for flat or stand-alone designs. Notice that the number of beads in each row will alternate plus or minus one bead. The mid-row looping technique is the same as in asymmetrical brick stitch; only the turns at the end of each row differ. Work the pattern from top to bottom as shown below.

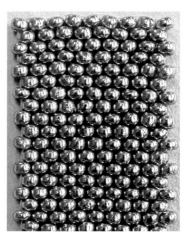

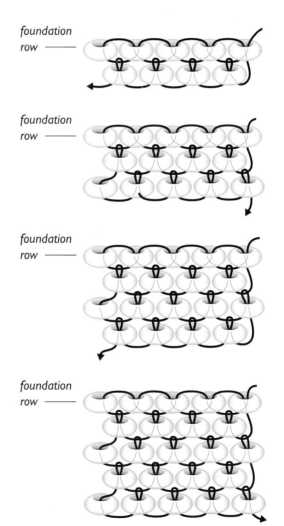

foundation row ———

foundation row ———

foundation row ———

foundation row ———

brick stitch increases

Increases are made at the beginning and end of each row as shown. The basic concept in increasing is to add beads in the same manner as the single-needle foundation row. When increasing on the right side, work the thread back through the added beads until it emerges from the bottom of the first bead added, then proceed through the rest of the row. Add beads on the left in a similar manner, again making certain that the thread emerges from the bottom of the last bead in the row.

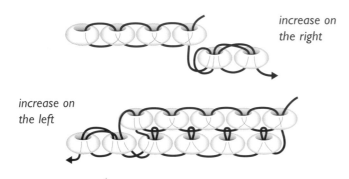

increase on the right

increase on the left

brick stitch decreases

Decreases on the right are made by working the thread back through beads on the end of the row until the thread emerges in proper position to continue as charted. To decrease on the left, simply end the row in the indicated position and bring the thread out of the bottom of the last bead, so the next row can be started.

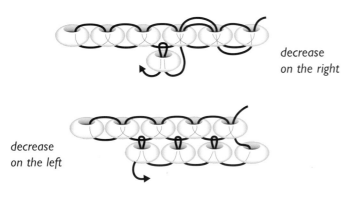

decrease on the right

decrease on the left

brick stitch with bugle beads

Bugle beads work up beautifully in brick stitch; the one concern is that bugle beads tend to have very sharp edges. This can be addressed by using an appropriate thread. If you use a lightweight thread, it should be doubled. Select bugle beads with good-sized holes because the weight of the thread will cause buildup within the hole. Many colors of silver-lined bugle beads come with square holes, which are excellent for this technique.

Begin with a single-needle ladder. Loop through the beads as shown until the first row is complete.

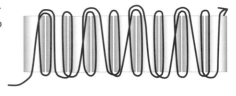

If the next row of the pattern calls for a decrease, work as shown, applying only one bead on the needle as you begin the row. Turn the work upon reaching the end of the row

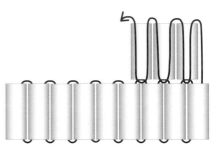

so you can continue to work with your dominant hand.

If the next row calls for an increase, put the first two beads on the needle, then loop as shown. Adjust the first two beads so they lie next to each other neatly.

When the row ends with an increase, loop back into the previous loop as shown. You may want to loop through the last two beads again

for stability before proceeding to the next row.

peyote stitch

Peyote stitch is one of the most popular beading techniques. It is strong and flexible, and it can be shaped by increasing or decreasing to fit a specific item. Designs are worked in rows from a chart. It works up quickly once the pattern has been established.

The first two rows of any peyote stitch design are threaded onto the needle at the same time. Thereafter, each individual row is added. The first bead you will place on the needle is from Row 2. Following the pattern shown, thread on the first two rows.

After you have put the beads on the thread, they will look like one long straight row. If you are weaving a piece less than 2" in width, you can stabilize the first two rows by placing the beads of Row 1 onto a head pin as shown. If you are working a longer piece, you should tape the end of your thread to a flat surface to help stabilize it.

Following the path of the thread as shown, add the beads of Row 3. If you are using a head pin, the first three rows should have a relatively neat appearance.

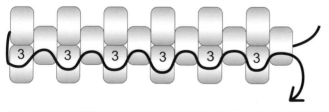

Row 4 is added in the same manner as Row 3.

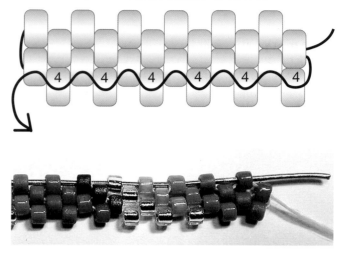

After Row 4, the stabilizing head pin is no longer needed, as the weave will be stable enough on its own to handle. Cross out rows in your chart as you progress to avoid confusion.

peyote stitch increases

If your chart calls for an increase, work the weave as shown, adding the beads at the beginning or end of the row. Until another bead is worked into an increase bead, it may flop around a bit. It will settle into place when anchored with another bead.

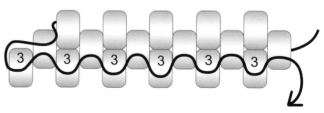

peyote stitch decreases

When the chart requires a decrease in the number of beads on a row, work the weave as shown. As in rows where increases are made, the end beads may want to misbehave. As the work progresses, the weave will stabilize. Decreases may be made at either end of a row in the same manner.

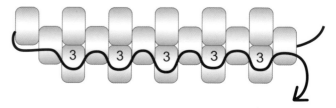

bargello bookmark

a bugle ladder

essentially provides the
foundation for this piece.
Additional ladders are
formed and attached to the
work using the brick stitch
method. The design, made
up of three shades of topaz,
incorporates decreases at
each end to form the points
and is embellished with
matte dark blue seed beads.
The bookmark is flexible,
yet sturdy enough to hold
the place in the book where
you left off until you can
take it up again. This quick
and easy-to-make piece is
a wonderful gift for both
the serious and the casual
readers on your list.

bargello bookmark chart

foundation row ———

bead code

![dark blue]	![seed beads]	11o Seed beads: matte dark blue (18)
![light]	![bugle]	#2 Bugle beads: matte light topaz AB (66)
![medium]	![bugle]	matte medium topaz (64)
![dark]	![bugle]	matte dark topaz (66)
![green]	![bugle]	silver-lined light green (140)

materials

Beads as listed in bead code
Thread, medium-weight: off-white

instructions

1 Refer to Brick Stitch with Bugle Beads on page 90. Begin at the center of the Bargello Bookmark Chart and create the foundation row, or a nine-bugle ladder, using two needles as shown.

2 Drop one thread at the end of the first ladder (dormant thread) and add additional ladders as shown, by looping through the threads on the previous ladder.

3 Continue in this manner, following the chart.

4 When you reach the peaks, decrease as shown, adding 11o seed beads. ·

5 When one end of the bookmark is complete, pick up the dormant thread, and weave out to the other end in the same manner.

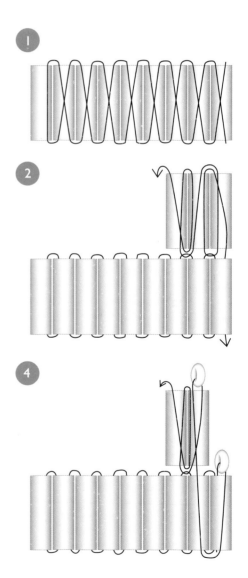

triangle necklace

woven entirely of one color and consisting of precisely ten rows of triangle beads,

there is no pattern for this piece. However, it is very easy to make using the peyote stitch method.

The triangle shapes fit neatly together once the weave is rolled into a tube. To accent the necklace, a

large bead made of amber was selected. For a textured effect, try alternating rows of matte gold and

bright gold beads.

materials

Beads
Large central stone or drop: amber
11o Seed bead: metallic gold (1)
8o Triangle beads, Toho 557 galvanized bright gold (14 grams)

Other materials
End crimps
Separating clasp
Thread, lightweight: off-white
Tigertail wire, medium-weight: 2" longer than the neck
    lace length

instructions

1 Refer to Peyote Stitch on page 91. Weave a strip of triangle
  beads to the desired length of the necklace. The strip
  should consist of precisely ten rows. Notice that the strip
  will not be neat and flat as it would be if it were woven in
  delicas or seed beads.

2 Form a tube from the flat weave.

  a. Roll the strip into a tube by gently forming it with
  your fingers.

  b. Join the edges along the entire length as shown.

  c. When the tube is complete the points of the triangles
  will point toward each other in the center.

3 Attach one side of the clasp to one end of the tigertail
  wire using a crimp. Carefully thread the tigertail through
  the length of the tube. Attach the other side of the clasp to
  the remaining end of the tigertail with the crimp, taking up
  the slack. Trim the excess tigertail to less than ½", then
  force the cut end of tigertail into the tube to conceal it.

4 Attach a thread near the center of the length of the tube
  and bring it out at the precise center of the tube. Add your
  drop bead plus the 11o seed bead. Run the thread back
  through the drop bead. Weave the attaching thread back
  into the tube until it is very secure, then clip the end.

1

2a

2b

2c

wave pendant

earth-toned

beads and leather cord combine for a very natural-looking piece. This three-dimensional pendant is worked in brick stitch. Two bands are created separately, the base band in 11o seed beads and the waved band in 15o seed beads. The two bands are joined at the top. The narrower band is "waved" and tacked into position. A single freshwater pearl hangs from its base. You can create this pendant in almost any combination of colors. This design can also be used for making drop earrings.

bead code

15o Seed beads:

Miyuki 403A opaque pale salmon (51)

Miyuki 403C opaque medium salmon (54)

Miyuki 409A opaque medium rust (61)

Miyuki 409 opaque dark rust (66)

Miyuki 277 metallic gold (28)

11o Seed beads, metallic gold (233)

Freshwater pearl, 5.5mm–6mm

materials

Beads as listed in bead code
Clasp
End crimps (2)
Leather cord, lightweight, 16"
Thread, medium-weight: off-white

base band chart

foundation row

1a

instructions

1 Refer to Brick Stitch on page 88. Work each band separately.

a. Work the base band according to Base Band Chart at right.

b. Work the waved band according to Waved Band Chart below.

1b

waved band chart

foundation row

2 Attach the pearl at the point of the narrow band, anchoring it with 11o metallic gold seed beads as shown.

3 Join bands together at their top edges with invisible stitches as shown. Notice that the weave runs in opposite directions when the bands are joined.

4 Position the narrow band in waves as shown. Tack the waves in position with invisible stitches.

Note: The photo shows a square bead instead of a pearl attached to the point of the narrow band.

5 Slip the leather cord through the space between the two bands at the top of the pendant.

6 Attach end crimps and the clasp at each end of the leather cord.

hex beaded necklace

less is more

as far as this design is concerned. Because there is one central design made of glinting hex beads, attention is immediately drawn to it. For this project, you will use the same technique that you learned for completing the Triangle Necklace on page 94 to assemble the gold side beads. You will make your first "beaded bead"— an experience that will prepare you for making several more when you are ready to craft either the Turquoise Necklace on page 104 or the Pink Crystals Necklace on page 108.

bead code

15o Hex beads:
    Toho 457C metallic copper (120)

    Toho 471 galvanized bright gold (40)

    Toho 706 matte metallic aqua iris (120)

    Miyuki 421A or Toho 122 opaque lustered
    ivory (150)

11o Seed beads:
    Miyuki 466 or Toho 224 metallic copper (240)

6mm Fire-polished crystals, galvanized gold (4)

8o Triangle beads, Toho 557 galvanized bright
gold (140)

materials

Beads as listed in bead code
Copier paper, 8½" x 11" (1 sheet)
End crimps to match the clasp (2)
Medium-gauge coated wire for necklace (18")
Separating clasp
Thread, lightweight: off-white
Transparent tape
Wire cutters

hex beaded necklace chart

instructions

1 Refer to Peyote Stitch on page 91. Work the design according to Hex Beaded Necklace Chart. Cut a piece of thread approximately 30" long and tape one end to a flat surface to facilitate handling. At some point within the weave, you will need to attach another thread; use a square knot and attach a piece approximately 30" long. Any excess left after weaving will be used in finishing. Leave a starting end of the thread at least 6".

2 Create the beaded bead by wrapping the beaded piece around a paper core:

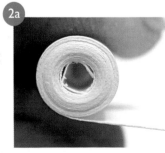

a. To form the bead's paper core, cut a strip of paper ⅝" wide. Leaving a small opening (⅛"), roll the strip between your fingers until it forms a solid tube. Make certain the tube is tightly wound. Using a small piece of tape, secure the tube. Add strips of paper and continue rolling until the diameter of the tube is approximately ⁷⁄₁₆" (1 cm). Take care to maintain the roundness of the tubular shape.

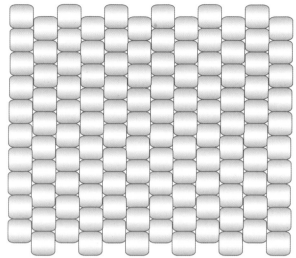

b. Wrap the beaded piece around the paper core. Using the excess thread ends of the original weave, join the edges together, fitting each bead snugly against the one to which it is joined to create the impression of a continuous weave. You may use a small piece of tape (to be removed later) to hold the edges together while you make the first few stitches. When the tube is secure and the joint well-hidden, bury the excess thread within the weave and clip close.

c. Add 15o ivory hex beads to both ends of the tube so all but the hole of the core is covered. Work each round as shown, making certain your thread tension is even and taut. Run a second loop of thread through the last round, then work the thread back through the bead to the other side. Repeat the end weaving, then bury the excess thread in the weave of the bead. Make certain the thread is secure before clipping.

2c

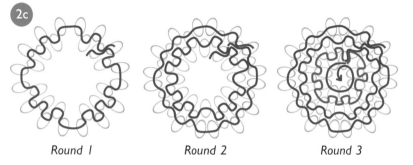

Round 1	*Round 2*	*Round 3*

beaded-bead blank
Use this blank to create your own beaded-bead design.

3 Weave the two tube beads with triangle beads according to Tube Beads Chart.

Note: The weave will not lie well because of the triangular shape of the beads used. However, when you have completed the weave, you will be able to roll it into a neat tube with matching edges.

4 Refer to Triangle Necklace Step 2 on page 95. Join the edges together so you have two tubular beads.

5 Assemble the necklace as follows: place the hex beaded-bead on the wire, then build outward on both sides by adding one gold 6mm crystal, then the triangle tube bead, then another 6mm crystal. Add 11o seed beads to create the desired length.

6 Add clasps to the necklace ends with end crimps. Slip the excess wire through the first few beads and pull to take up the slack before tightening the crimp. Trim excess wire with wire cutters.

egyptian brooch

inspired by a beautiful piece displayed in the Museum of Fine Arts in Boston, this piece is a combination of

11o seed beads worked up in brick stitch and faux turquoise oval drop beads. A pin back was attached to the

back of the piece so it can be worn on a jacket lapel or shirt collar. The original piece was smaller and made

of faience beads (hard-baked clay with a matte finish). It was part of the burial treasure for a minor Egyptian

princess who lived and died circa 2000 B.C.

bead code

11o Seed beads:
Czech opaque matte aqua AB (88)

Czech opaque bone (60)

Czech galvanized gold (76)

4mm Square galvanized gold (6)

6mm x 9mm Oval drop beads, faux turquoise (3)

materials

Beads as listed in bead code
Pin back, 1¼"
Thread, lightweight: off-white

instructions

1 Refer to Brick Stitch on page 88. Work the design according to Egyptian Brooch Chart.

2 Add beaded drops to lower edge of design.

   a. Bring the thread out in the proper position (according to the chart) to create the right drop.

   b. Add the beads as diagrammed, skip the last 11o gold galvanized, then run the thread back through all the beads on the drop.

   c. Weave the thread through the completed design, then bring it out in position to begin the center drop. Continue in this manner until all three drops are formed.

   d. Bury the thread in the design.

3 Sew the pin back in place with invisible stitches.

egyptian brooch chart

foundation row ——

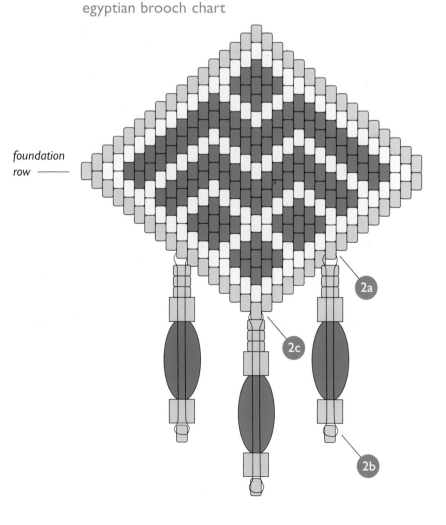

turquoise combination

a perfect pair, the turquoise necklace and earrings make a very natural statement. Although these pieces look complex, they are actually quite easy to do. Simply create each beaded bead, using the brick stitch method and string them together with fire-polished crystals, turquoise disks, and 11o seed beads. For a more chic effect, try using semi-precious-stone beads in different shapes between the beaded beads. Play with the color combinations to coordinate with that trendy new outfit that needs just the right accessories.

materials

Beads as listed in bead code
Copier paper, 8½" x 11" (3 sheets)
Ear wires for earrings (2)
End crimps to match the clasp (2)
Head pins for earrings, 1½" (2)
Medium-gauge coated wire for necklace (15")
Round-nosed pliers
Separating clasp for necklace
Thread, lightweight: off-white
Transparent tape
Wire cutters

instructions

1 Refer to Asymmetrical Brick Stitch on page 89. Work the designs according to Turquoise Combination Necklace & Earring Charts on page 107. Cut a piece of thread approximately 30" long and tape one end to a flat surface to facilitate handling. At some point within the weave, you will need to attach another thread; use a square knot and attach a piece approximately 30" long. Any excess left after weaving will be used in finishing. Leave a starting end of the thread at least 6". Make four of Bead 1, three of Bead 2, and two of Bead 3. Make two of the earring pattern.

2 Create a beaded bead by wrapping the beaded piece around a paper core:

a. To form the bead's paper core, cut a strip of paper ⅝" wide. Leaving a small opening (⅛"), roll the strip between your fingers until

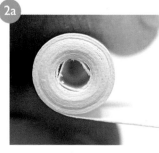

it forms a solid tube. Make certain the tube is tightly wound. Using a small piece of tape, secure the tube. Add strips of paper and

bead code

Delica beads:
  Miyuki 335 matte silver (1484)

Miyuki 374 matte seafoam (1552)

Miyuki 22 metallic bronze (732)

11o Seed beads: Toho 558 F matte silver (50)

6mm Fire-polished crystals, bronze for necklace only (26)

10mm Fire-polished crystals, bronze for earrings only (4)

15mm Flat turquoise disks with center hole (18)

continue rolling until the diameter of the tube is approximately ⁷⁄₁₆" (1 cm). Take care to maintain the roundness of the tubular shape. Repeat to make nine paper cores for the necklace and two for the earrings.

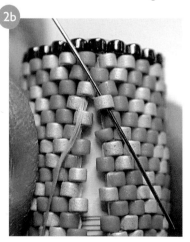

b. Wrap each beaded piece around a paper core. Using the excess thread ends of the original weave, join the edges together, fitting each bead snugly against the one to which it is joined to create the impression of a continuous weave. You may use a small piece of tape (to be removed later) to hold the edges together while you make the first few stitches. When the tube is secure and the joint well-hidden, bury the excess thread within the weave and clip the thread close.

3 Assemble the necklace according to Necklace Assembly. Review the detail to see how the turquoise disks, beaded beads, crystals, and 11o seed beads fit together.

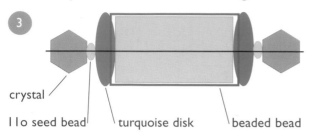

crystal

11o seed bead — turquoise disk — beaded bead

Bead 1 assembly

Bead 2 assembly

Bead 3 assembly

4 Add clasps to the necklace ends with crimps. Slip the excess wire through the first few beads and pull to take up the slack before tightening the crimp. Trim excess wire with wire cutters.

necklace assembly

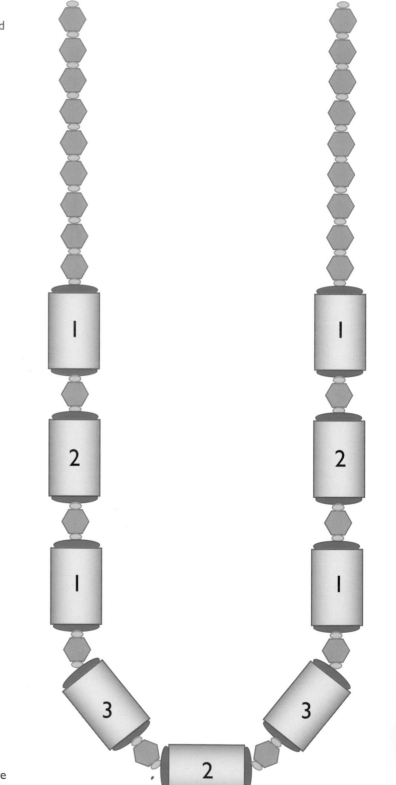

turquoise combination necklace chart — bead 1

5 Assemble the earrings as shown. Trim the excess head pin to ⅜" (.8 cm) and turn a loop using round-nosed pliers, leaving a gap sufficient to fit over the loop on the ear wire. Join the assembly to the ear wire and close the gap.

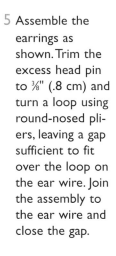

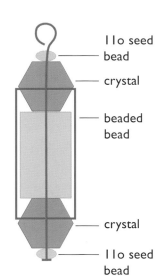

11o seed bead

crystal

beaded bead

crystal

11o seed bead

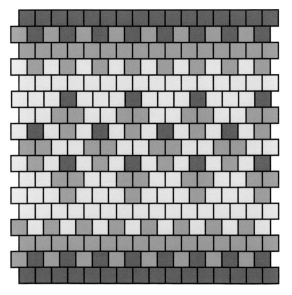

Earring assembly

turquoise combination necklace chart — bead 2

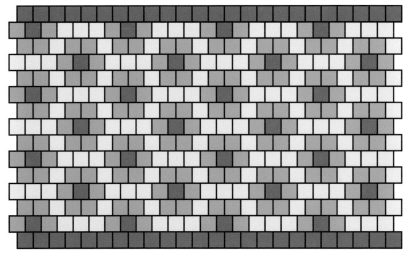

turquoise combination earrings chart

turquoise combination necklace chart — bead 3

pink crystals necklace

symmetry,

pure and simple, is the key

ingredient to the stunning

design for this necklace. It is

created with eleven beaded

beads woven in 150 seed

beads, using the brick stitch

method. These beads are

strung together with pink

crystal spacers and 60 seed

beads. Though they are

similar to the beaded beads

created in the Turquoise

Combination necklace and

earrings on page 104, the

beads in this project go one

step further—almost

completely enclosing the

paper tube around which

they are wrapped.

bead code

150 Seed beads:

Miyuki 401 or Toho 49 opaque black (1392)

Miyuki 406C opaque dark brick red (76)

Miyuki 403C opaque medium brick red (412)

Miyuki 403B opaque light salmon (288)

Miyuki 2023 matte opaque pink (2232)

60 Seed beads: Miyuki 410 or Toho 49 opaque black (30)

6mm Faceted beads, rose quartz (18)

materials

Beads as listed in bead code
Copier paper, 8½" x 11" (3 sheets)
End crimps to match the clasp (2)
Medium-gauge coated wire for necklace (18")
Separating clasp
Thread, lightweight: off-white
Transparent tape
Wire cutters

instructions

1 Refer to Brick Stitch on page 88. Work the designs according to Pink Crystals Necklace Charts on pages 111–112. Cut a piece of thread approximately 30" long and tape one end to a flat surface to facilitate handling. At some point within the weave, you will need to attach another thread; use a square knot and attach a piece approximately 30" long. Any excess left after weaving will be used in finishing. Leave a starting end of the thread at least 6". Make one of Bead 1, make two of all other beads.

2 Create a beaded bead by wrapping the beaded piece around a paper core:

a. To form the bead's paper core, cut two ¾" x 9½" strips of paper. Join the two strips with a small piece of clear tape that does not extend beyond the edges of the paper, to create a single ¾" x 19" strip. Leaving a small opening (¹⁄₁₆"), roll the strip between your fingers until it forms a solid tube. Make certain the tube is tightly wound. When you near the end of the strip, place a small spot of glue approximately 1" away from the end and spread it toward the end of the strip. Allow to dry.

2a

Use a piece of tape to secure the tube as it dries.

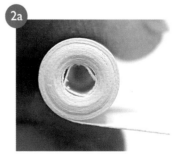

If necessary, color the surface of the core with a magic marker so it coordinates with the color or colors of the beaded piece. Repeat to make eleven paper cores.

b. Wrap each beaded piece around a paper core so the even edges are together. If the core is too large, peel back a bit of the paper until it is the correct size. If it is too small, add a small strip of paper to enlarge it. Using the excess thread ends of the original weave, join the edges together, fitting each bead snugly against the one to which it is joined to create the impression of a continuous weave. You may use a small piece of tape (to be removed later) to hold the edges together while you make the first few stitches. When the tube is secure and the joint well-hidden, bury the excess thread within the weave and clip the thread close.

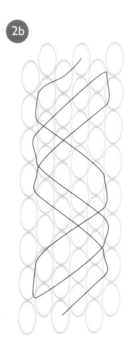

c. Add beads to both ends of the tube so all but the hole of the core is covered. Work each round as shown in the photo and diagrams, making certain your thread tension is even and taut. Run a second loop of thread through the last round, then work the thread back through the bead to the other side. Repeat the end weaving, then bury the excess thread in the weave of the bead. Make certain the thread is secure before clipping. Finish all eleven beads in the same manner.

Note: The diagrams show the sequential method used to weave the tube ends closed. The lavender beads in the example chart represent the lavender beads in the diagrams; the photo shows the work in progress.

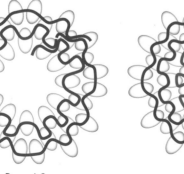

Lavender beads indicate those that start the end weave.

Round 1

Round 2

Round 3

③

6 · **3** · **4** · **2** · **5** · **1** · **5** · **2** · **4** · **3** · **6**

3 Assemble the necklace as shown.

④

4 Add clasps to the necklace ends with crimps. Slip the excess wire through the first few beads and pull to take up the slack before tightening the crimp. Trim excess wire with wire cutters.

Note: These charts may also be woven in Peyote Stitch by rotating them 90 degrees.

pink crystals necklace chart — bead 1

pink crystals necklace chart — bead 2

pink crystals necklace chart — bead 3

pink crystals necklace chart — bead 5

pink crystals necklace chart — bead 4

pink crystals necklace chart — bead 6

beaded bead blanks   Use these blanks to create your own beaded-bead designs.

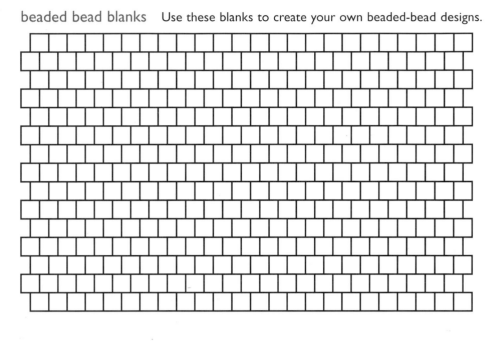

alternate design

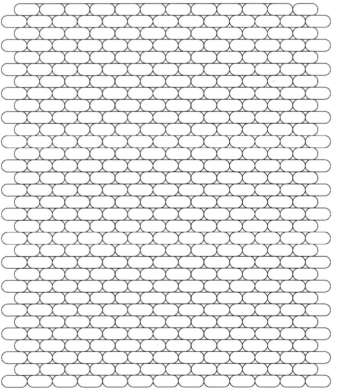

needle cases

treasures, as well as needles, can be kept in these small, sweet cases. They can be made up using either the peyote stitch method or the brick stitch method. Each consists of a flat-weave pattern that is wrapped around a tubular case and joined at the edges. The ends are finished by beading individual rounds until the space is filled. Personalize your needle case by adding on a fringe or drop bead. Suspend your needle case from a beaded chain for easy access to your sewing needles.

materials

Beads as listed in bead code
Thread, lightweight nylon: off-white
Tubular wooden needle case with removable
  top, ½" diameter, 3⅛" long
White glue

bead code

15o Seed beads:
  Toho 617 matte metallic olive (340)

Miyuki 411G opaque olive (275)

Miyuki 1889 gold-lustered medium olive (340)

Toho 762 matte opaque cream (375)

Miyuki F471A matte galvanized gold (320)

diamond needle case instructions

Note: Tubular needle cases with removable tops are available in somewhat standard sizes. Most have an outside diameter of ½". Woven patterns can be worked to fit around the outside of these cases, with very attractive results. The patterns in this book are intended for ½"-diameter cases; they may be adjusted for the length of your needle case.

1 Refer to Peyote Stitch on page 91. Work design according to Diamond Needle Case Chart on page 117.

2 Fit the finished beadwork around the needle case and make any necessary adjustments.

Note: There are multiple variables in the beading process that may affect the final size of your woven piece. Most are not determinable ahead of time. They include:

• *Your stitch tension. If you pull the thread tightly, the finished piece will be slightly smaller than the sample, and if your tension is loose, it will be larger. If you are aware of your tension being too tight or too loose, try to adjust it. If your pattern is not geometric, you may be able to eliminate or add one row to make an adjustment. If the nature of the pattern makes that undesirable, you can make adjustments in the size of the tube itself.*

• *The natural variation in the size of the beads. This is not as much of a problem with tube beads such as delicas, but with seed beads there is often a slight variation from color to color.*

• *Slight variations in the diameter of the tube. In some cases, the milling may result in a minutely larger or smaller diameter for the tube, which will result in a difference in the fit of the pattern. If the tube is too large, sand it with a fine-gauge sandpaper. You would be surprised how quickly the diameter of the tube can be reduced. If it is too small, pad it out with a couple of layers of masking tape. Use tape that is wider than the circumference of the tube; lay it on carefully to avoid wrinkles. If necessary, the edges can be trimmed with scissors to minimize the visibility of the tape. Add one layer at a time until the fit is correct.*

3 Join the edges together as shown.

Note: The main body of the tube will probably not need any glue to hold the woven beadwork in place. However, if desired, you can secure it before joining the edges together with a very thin layer of glue. Complete the joining before the glue dries.

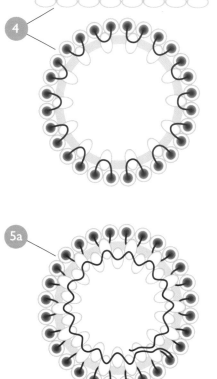

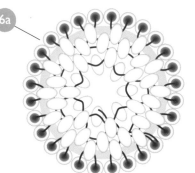

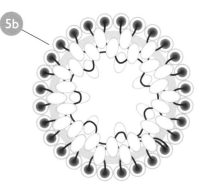

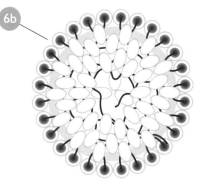

4 Bring the thread out in any bead on the bottom edge, then add matte opaque cream beads all around that edge as shown. You will have a total of 14 new beads in that round.

5 Add the next round as shown, then two more rounds as shown.

6 Fill in the remaining gap with beads as shown. Notice that there is room for one more bead. Bury any excess thread ends within the weave and clip carefully.

7

8a

7 To weave the cap design, work the first eight vertical rows as indicated from the right side of the Diamond Needle Case Chart.

8 Cover the cap.

a. Apply a thin layer of glue to the cap as shown.

b. Repeat Steps 2–6 on pages 115–116 for the top of the cap in the same manner as the for the bottom of the tube, but with matte galvanized gold beads.

Note: If desired, fringes and hangers may be added to the main body of the tube.

bead code

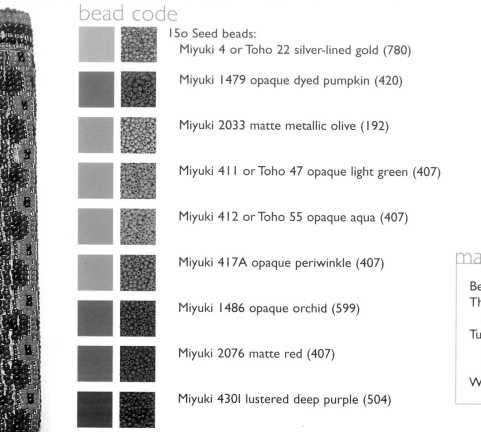

15o Seed beads:

Miyuki 4 or Toho 22 silver-lined gold (780)

Miyuki 1479 opaque dyed pumpkin (420)

Miyuki 2033 matte metallic olive (192)

Miyuki 411 or Toho 47 opaque light green (407)

Miyuki 412 or Toho 55 opaque aqua (407)

Miyuki 417A opaque periwinkle (407)

Miyuki 1486 opaque orchid (599)

Miyuki 2076 matte red (407)

Miyuki 4301 lustered deep purple (504)

materials

Beads as listed in bead code
Thread, lightweight nylon:
    off-white
Tubular wooden needle case
    with removable top,
    ½" diameter, 3⅛" long
White glue

watercolor needle case instructions

1 Refer to Brick Stitch on page 88. Work design according to Watercolor Needle Case Chart on page 119.

2 Fit the finished beadwork around the needle case so the even edges are together and make any necessary adjustments. Using the excess thread ends of the original weave, join the edges together, fitting each bead snugly against the one to which it is joined to create the impression of a continuous weave. You may use a small piece of tape (to be removed later) to hold the edges together while you make the first few stitches. When the tube is secure and the joint well-hidden, bury the excess thread within the weave and clip the thread close.

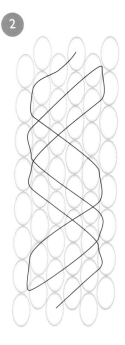

3 To finish the bottom edge, repeat Steps 4–6 for Diamond Needle Case on page 116 with silver-lined gold beads.

4 To weave the cap design, work eight horizontal rows, in the following order: a row of opaque dyed pumpkin, a row of opaque light green, a row of opaque aqua, a row of opaque orchid, a row of matte red, a row of silver-lined gold, a row of lustered deep purple, and a row of silver-lined gold.

5 To cover cap, repeat Step 8 for Diamond Needle Case on page 117 with silver-lined gold beads.

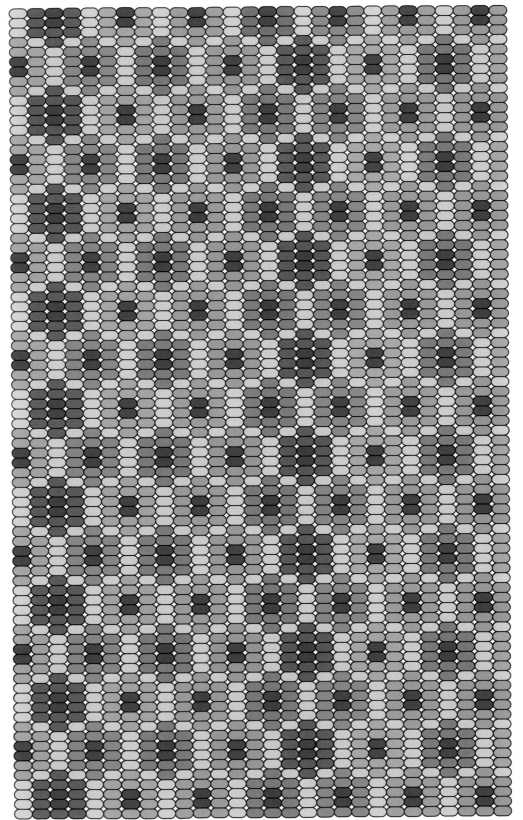

needle case blank — peyote stitch   Use this blank to create your own design.

needle case blank — brick stitch   Use this blank to create your own design.

bargello lamp shade

six panels

are individually woven and joined together to create this expensive-looking piece. The Bargello Lamp Shade is certainly an impressive project. However, because brick stitching in bugle beads works up quickly, it does not take as much time as you would think. Simply slip it over a small metal shade frame, add a base and bulb, and you have a charming new home accessory. This piece can be easily customized to the color scheme of any room's decor by substituting the colors listed in the bead code on page 123.

122

bead code

#2 Czech bugle beads
silver-lined bronze AB (1740)

matte medium aqua AB (648)

matte light lavender AB (552)

matte medium sapphire AB (600)

matte light topaz AB (540)

15o Seed beads: Miyuki 2025, matte opaque light amethyst (912)

Fire-polished crystals, topaz: 10mm (6); 6mm (12); 4mm (18) (not shown)

materials

Beads as listed in bead code
Lamp shade frame, hexagonal, 3" top x 5" bottom
   x 4" high
Thread, medium-weight: off-white

instructions

Note: This piece was designed for use with Czech #2 bugle beads. Japanese beads are sized slightly different from Czech and will not work, as the size of the finished panel will not be correct for the lamp-shade frame. Also notice that the length of the shade is slightly longer than the frame and the beading will extend slightly beyond the bottom of the frame.

1 Refer to Brick Stitch with Bugle Beads on page 90. Work design according to Bargello Lamp Shade Chart on page 124. Repeat for six individual panels.

Note: If a bead is significantly longer than others in the weave, it will create puckering. While some slight variation is expected and acceptable, the light topaz bead in the top row shown is too long and should not be used.

2 Join the panels together by weaving the edges as shown.

Note: Where the panels are shaped by decreases, the joint will not appear smooth at first. Do not be concerned about this. When the beading is placed on the lamp-shade frame, the joints will smooth out and the shaping will be less noticeable.

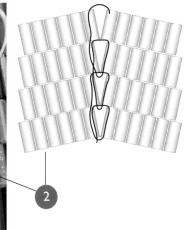

3 After the panels are joined, add the upper and lower edging as shown.

Note: At this point, you can switch to a lighter-weight thread that will slip more easily through the 15o beads.

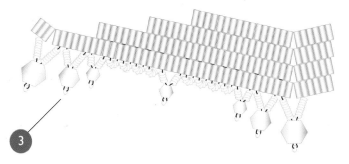

123

bargello lamp shade chart

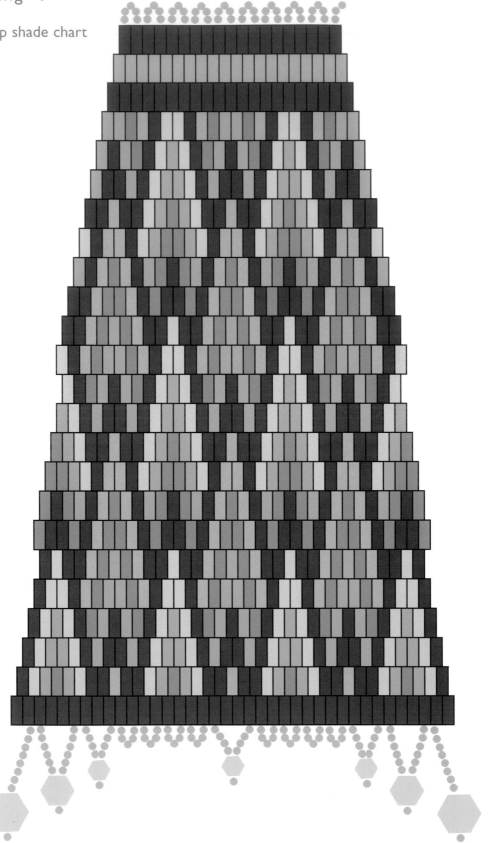

bargello lamp shade blank
Use this blank to create
your own design.

photo courtesy of Bertelsman Publishing

about the author

Ann Benson is the author of seven books on beading including the best-selling titles *Two-Hour Beaded Projects*, *Beadweaving*, and *Beadpoint*.

"My love of beads knows no limit. It's been my passion for 25 years. I especially love seed beads—the range of colors is so astonishing!"

Ms. Benson is also the author of four historical novels, including the acclaimed Plague Trilogy, beginning with *The Plague Tales* (Delacorte Press, 1997), which is taught as part of multidisciplinary units in many public and private schools.

Her two grown daughters, Meryl and Ariel, are a source of constant joy and inspiration to her.

Ann also owns and operates Beads East, a retail bead store in Vernon, Connecticut, near where she resides with her beloved husband Gary. Please visit the store when you are traveling in the New England area. Visit her web sites, too, at www.annbenson.com or www.beadseast.com.

dedication

This book is dedicated with love to the memory of Jane Gallagher Ritson.

metric equivalency chart

inches to millimetres and centimetres (mm-millimetres   cm-centimetres)

inches	mm	cm	inches	cm	inches	cm	inches	cm
⅛	3	0.3	6	15.2	21	53.3	36	91.4
¼	6	0.6	7	17.8	22	55.9	37	94.0
⅜	10	1.0	8	20.3	23	58.4	38	96.5
½	13	1.3	9	22.9	24	61.0	39	99.1
⅝	16	1.6	10	25.4	25	63.5	40	101.6
¾	19	1.9	11	27.9	26	66.0	41	104.1
⅞	22	2.2	12	30.5	27	68.6	42	106.7
1	25	2.5	13	33.0	28	71.1	43	109.2
1¼	32	3.2	14	35.6	29	73.7	44	111.8
1½	38	3.8	15	38.1	30	76.2	45	114.3
1¾	44	4.4	16	40.6	31	78.7	46	116.8
2	51	5.1	17	43.2	32	81.3	47	119.4
3	76	7.6	18	45.7	33	83.8	48	121.9
4	102	10.2	19	48.3	34	86.4	49	124.5
5	127	12.7	20	50.8	35	88.9	50	127.0

index

a–b

Adding a new length of thread 12
Asymmetrical brick stitch. 89
Bargello Bookmark. 92–93
Bargello Lamp Shade. 122–125
Beading tips 15
Bead colors 11
Beads 8–11
Black Lace Necklace. 40–42
Brick stitch. 88–90
Brick stitch decreases. 90
Brick stitch increases 90
Brick stitch with bugle beads 90
Bridal Bag. 43–49
Bridal Necklace 51–53
Brooch blanks 15
Bugle beads. 9, 17
Bugle Earrings. 54–55

c–d

Camellias 70–75
Caps. 15
Card stock versus nonwoven fabric 16
Choosing a fiber. 12
Clasps 15
Cloisonné beads. 9
Coaster 36–37
Counting beads 15
Create the foundation row 32
Crimps. 13
Crystals and other faceted beads. 18
Delica seed beads 8
Designs can be worked in rounds 35
Diamond Needle Case 115–117
Dillon, Ann. 82
Dimensional Sunflowers 29–31
Double-needle foundation row 88

e–g

Ear findings. 15
Egyptian Brooch. 102–103
Eye pins 15
Faceted crystal beads. 9
Fancy glass beads 9
Figuring needed amounts 11
Filet beading. 32–49
Filet beading chart 32
Filet beading primer 32–35
Filet-beading decreases. 35
Filet-beading increases 35
Finishing surface beading 18
First row is complete, The 34
Freshwater pearls. 18
Garden Sunset 76–80
Getting Started. 8–15

h–k

Head pins. 15
Heart Ornament 38–39
Hex Beaded Necklace 99–101
Hex seed beads 8
If the first pat in the new row is filled 34
If the first pat in the new row is open 34
If the first pat is filled 33
If the first pat is open. 32
If the next pat is filled 33
If the next pat is open 33
Irish Sunset. 22–24
Jewelry components. 13–15
Jumping beads 15
Kilim Rug 64–69
Kimono 81–87

l–m

Ladder bead-weaving 50–61
Ladder bead-weaving primer 50
Larger seed beads 17
Length of thread. 12
Loom bead-weaving 62–87
Loom bead-weaving primer 62–63
Looms 62
Lovers, The. 20–21
Medieval Castle 25–28
Metal beads 9
Methods for transferring the design 16
Metric equivalency chart 127

n–p

Natural beads. 10
Needle Cases 114–121
Needle-weaving 88–125
Needle-weaving primer 88–91
Needles 13
Organization 15
Peridot Bracelet. 53
Peyote stitch 91
Peyote stitch decreases 91
Peyote stitch increases 91
Pink Crystals Necklace 108–113
Pliers 13
Purse frames 15
Pyramids Bracelet. 56–57

r–s

Rainbow Bracelet 58–61
Removing beads. 15
Rings 15
Seed beads. 8
Semiprecious-stone chips 17
Sewing on seed beads. 16–17
Single-needle foundation row 88
Spilled beads. 15
Surface beading. 16–31
Surface beading primer. 16–19
Symmetrical brick stitch. 89

t–w

Thread 12
Three-cut seed beads. 8–9
To complete the rows with filled and open pats. 35
Tools 13
Triangle Necklace. 94–95
Turquoise Combination 104–107
Variations on a ladder 50
Warp 63
Watercolors Needle Case 118–119
Wave Pendant. 96–98
Weaving a basic ladder. 50
Weaving the design 63
Weft. 63
Wire cutters 13